And Came the Spring

A Comedy of Modern Youth in Three Acts

by Marrijane and Joseph Hayes

A SAMUEL FRENCH ACTING EDITION

New York Hollywood London Toronto
SAMUELFRENCH.COM

Copyright © 1942 by Samuel French

ALL RIGHTS RESERVED

CAUTION: Professionals and amateurs are hereby warned that *AND CAME THE SPRING* is subject to a Licensing Fee. It is fully protected under the copyright laws of the United States of America, the British Commonwealth, including Canada, and all other countries of the Copyright Union. All rights, including professional, amateur, motion picture, recitation, lecturing, public reading, radio broadcasting, television and the rights of translation into foreign languages are strictly reserved. In its present form the play is dedicated to the reading public only.

The amateur live stage performance rights to *AND CAME THE SPRING* are controlled exclusively by Samuel French, Inc., and licensing arrangements and performance licenses must be secured well in advance of presentation. PLEASE NOTE that amateur Licensing Fees are set upon application in accordance with your producing circumstances. When applying for a licensing quotation and a performance license please give us the number of performances intended, dates of production, your seating capacity and admission fee. Licensing Fees are payable one week before the opening performance of the play to Samuel French, Inc., at 45 W. 25th Street, New York, NY 10010.

Licensing Fee of the required amount must be paid whether the play is presented for charity or gain and whether or not admission is charged.

Stock licensing fees quoted upon application to Samuel French, Inc.

For all other rights than those stipulated above, apply to: Samuel French, Inc.

Particular emphasis is laid on the question of amateur or professional readings, permission and terms for which must be secured in writing from Samuel French, Inc.

Copying from this book in whole or in part is strictly forbidden by law, and the right of performance is not transferable.

Whenever the play is produced the following notice must appear on all programs, printing and advertising for the play: "Produced by special arrangement with Samuel French, Inc."

Due authorship credit must be given on all programs, printing and advertising for the play.

No one shall commit or authorize any act or omission by which the copyright of, or the right to copyright, this play may be impaired.

No one shall make any changes in this play for the purpose of production.

Publication of this play does not imply availability for performance. Both amateurs and professionals considering a production are strongly advised in their own interests to apply to Samuel French, Inc., for written permission before starting rehearsals, advertising, or booking a theatre.

No part of this book may be reproduced, stored in a retrieval system, or transmitted in any form, by any means, now known or yet to be invented, including mechanical, electronic, photocopying, recording, videotaping, or otherwise, without the prior written permission of the publisher.

ISBN 978-0-573-60531-4   Printed in U.S.A.   #3069

AND CAME THE SPRING

STORY OF THE PLAY

And Came The Spring is the brightly humorous and straightforward story of the Hartmans, a pleasantly typical American family, who enjoy a reasonable amount of quiet and peace until Spring enters the scene—to stir the blood and lift the heart. On the first day of Spring vacation, Midge, the youngest, finds herself surprisingly in the throes of first love. A charming and lovable hoyden is Midge—complex, alive, and warmly human. She thinks nothing of starting whirlwinds or even tornadoes to impress casual, witty Buzz Lindsay, the young gentleman of her choice—who is unluckily in love with older sister Virginia. When the spirited Midge determines to manage lives and emotions for her own ends, the hectic and hilarious complications into which she plunges the family almost prove disastrous. She causes her sister to be suspected as a thief, to almost lose the right boy; she drops a bombshell into her father's business, threatening her sister's college education; she disrupts brilliant brother Elliott's carefully planned life as a writer of tragic novels; she plays havoc with the hearts of several other young people, including a visiting New York glamour girl and a bashful boy who really cares for Midge herself—in short, the sanity and well-being of everyone concerned. At the second act climax the world comes smashing down around an angered family and a bewildered—and remorseful—Midge. Mrs. Hartman is almost ready to admit that Mr. Hartman was right in contending that young people of today are more irresponsible than the youth of his day. But on the night of the Spring Prom — Midge's first formal dance — she steps in again and sets matters straight in a heart-warming and very funny manner. By the end of the week the three Hartman children have taken important steps toward maturity, and their parents have learned a few things too.

CHARACTERS

Mr. Jeffrey Hartman
Elliott Hartman
Buzz Lindsay
Keith Nolan
Freddie North
Mr. Fields
Alan Fields
Clancy
Messenger Boy
Mrs. Louise Hartman
Midge Hartman
Virginia Hartman
Carollyn Webster
Gabby Allen
Edna
Mrs. Fields
Christine Myers

ACTION AND SCENE

The entire action of the play takes place in the attractive living room of the Hartman home.

ACT ONE
    Scene 1. *About nine o'clock, a bright spring Monday morning.*

ACT TWO
    Scene 1. *Tuesday, immediatetly after dinner.*
    Scene 2. *About ten o'clock, Wednesday evening.*
    Scene 3. *Late Friday afternoon.*

ACT THREE. *Saturday evening, a little after eight o'clock.*

DESCRIPTIONS OF CHARACTERS

MIDGE HARTMAN—*Energetic, bright-eyed, healthy. She is an unrepressed 15 in every sense of the word. Her manner is a fascinating mixture of awkwardness and swift animal-like grace.*

VIRGINIA HARTMAN — *A slimly attractive young lady of the world, going on 18 and very conscious of her determination to be sophisticated. Has charm and a good spirit, with quick sympathies.*

ELLIOTT HARTMAN—*A tall, slender boy of 16 with hair that has rarely experienced a combing, although his character demands extreme neatness and precision—especially in regard to the emotions. He wears, when play begins, a rather dour expression—an expression which he is rather determined to maintain. His eyes are those of a poet, and he knows it. Elliott could be a very charming boy, and his transformation should be played to the hilt—contrasting his appearance at beginning of first act and at end of third.*

MRS. LOUISE HARTMAN—*Pleasant, tolerant, cheerful. An understanding woman in her 40s, often baffled by her children but never really doubting their innate sanity and worth. She has a relish and appreciation for their charms despite their often preplexing proximity.*

DESCRIPTION OF CHARACTERS

MR. JEFFREY HARTMAN—*A typical business man in appearance and a rather confused parent. In his 40s. His wisdom does not match that of his wife, but he rather enjoys his angry moments.*

EDNA, the maid—*An attractive woman of less than 30.*

CLANCY, the gardener—*A huge, gentle man with a broad, open face. About 32. He was once a college football hero, and in those days life was fairly simple.*

BUZZ LINDSAY — *An easy-going, casually dressed fellow of 17. Good-natured and possessing much unconscious charm. Understanding and likeable.*

CAROLLYN WEBSTER—*A young lady of 17. She is a New York glamour girl and as such has received a great deal of publicity. She tries very hard to live up to it and to make the right impression. Her long hair falls down the side of her face in the fashion of the times. She really wants to be liked by everyone. Her way of speaking (emphasis, etc.) is indicated in script.*

KEITH NOLAN—*Always extremely well-dressed. His manner is sometimes supercilious; his speech and gestures, choice of words and mannerisms betray the fact that he has ambitions of a theatrical nature. Perhaps he has read too much Noel Coward.*

GABBY ALLEN — *Extremely energetic 15. Dresses brightly. Rarely sits still. She is what is commonly referred to as a "jitterbug." All of her lines are spoken with awe and the utmost sincerity, and we feel that she not only enjoys most of what she does—she glories in life itself.*

FREDDIE NOLAN—*Gabby's male counterpart, same age. Like Gabby, he speaks his own language. Dresses in plaid shirts, bright ties, etc.*

DESCRIPTION OF CHARACTERS

MRS. CECELIA FIELDS—*Buxom woman in her 40s. Wears fluffy clothes which do not in any way suit her personality. Determined countenance.*

MR. LINK FIELDS—*A gentle be-mustached little man in his 40s. Small in stature, an excellent business man—rather obsequious in appearance and in manner until last Act. This change also should be played to the hilt.*

ALAN FIELDS—*Eighteen. Reticent, even occasionally awkward. Fresh open face and a winning manner. He is confused and embarrassed by his parents.*

MESSENGER BOY—*Any age. Flip and sharp. Wisecracks.*

CHRISTINE MYERS—*17. Dynamic, athletic, dressed roughly. She is school cheer-leader as well as captain of about every girl's athletic activity. She is the kind of a girl who, as cheer leader, somehow shakes a spectator's confidence in a team of mere boys. She walks with head jutting out in front, shoulders hunched over.*

And Came The Spring

ACT ONE

Scene I

Scene: *The Hartmans' living room, a warm-toned room graced with that lived-in atmosphere which pleasantly exists when a home is inhabited by three teen-aged young people and their parents and friends. It is in good taste and provides an attractive setting for the action which follows:*

In the Right wall are French doors which open onto a sun porch. In front of these doors is a desk on which the telephone rests and a straight chair is in back of the desk, facing downstage. Waste basket near desk. Against the Right rear wall is a stairway with a landing. On this landing is the door to Midge's room, which is set in a rear wall. Below the landing is an occasional table with a lamp on it. On the Right wall above the table is a mirror. In the Left rear wall is a window with straight chairs on either side and above each is a colorful print.

The upper Left corner in which the outside door is set is cut diagonally. When this door is opened, a porch railing comes into view. At Left Center the davenport is set at an angle and

*to the Right of it are a drum table, on which is
a lamp, and a lounge chair. The dining room
door is set in the Center of the Left wall. A
lounge chair facing up at an angle is down Left
in the corner and a radio is placed between the
outside and dining room doors. Above the radio
there is another mirror.*

TIME: *About nine o'clock, a bright spring Monday
morning.*

AT RISE: *A small card table has been set up down
Center; breakfast things are on the table.
Chairs Right, Left of table.* EDNA, *about 30,
in a crisp maid's uniform, is busy adding dishes
and silver to the table. She is humming tune-
lessly. There is a knock at the Left 2 door.
She opens it.* CLANCY, *the gardener, stands
there with the morning paper in his hand.*
CLANCY *is a huge, gentle man with a broad,
open, amiable face.*

EDNA. Oh—you. *(Returns and busies herself at
table.)*

CLANCY. Yeah, me.—Say, what are you dolled up
for?

EDNA. *(Taking paper; opening it on table.)* The
Hartmans are having a visitor—very important—
and they won't want the gardener in the living
room.

CLANCY. Edna, have you seen the sun?

EDNA. I'm much too busy to stand gaping at the
sun.

CLANCY. It's a real spring day. *(Goes to* EDNA,
places his hand on her shoulder.)

EDNA. Well, don't let that give you any ideas.

CLANCY. Gosh, Edna, when I was playing football in college, you should have seen the girls who came to see me in the locker room.

EDNA. You're not in college now, Clancy.

CLANCY. I still remember. — Sorority girls. *(MIDGE HARTMAN appears on landing — entering from her room. MIDGE is an unrepressed fifteen. She wears dirty saddle shoes, tennis shorts, and an open, healthy expression which can easily dissolve into the bewilderment of her age. She watches quiety a moment.)* I haven't forgotten, sister.

EDNA: And don't call me "sister."

CLANCY. Edna, you're afraid to admit you love me.

EDNA *(Simply, listlessly, sing-song.)* No, I'm not. I love you.—Now—go on out to the garden before Mr. Hartman fires you.

CLANCY. A kiss'd put me in the pink.

(MIDGE stealthily returns to her room.)

EDNA. Listen, Clancy, Mr. Hartman meant it. He said if he ever caught us together during working hours, he'd fire both of us.

CLANCY. Even Mr. Hartman would realize it's spring. On a day like this—*(Sniffs)* What's that stink?

EDNA. Paint. And it's not a stink, it's an odor. They're painting the dining room.

(MIDGE, with Kodak camera, returns to landing— camera trained on EDNA and CLANCY.)

CLANCY. That means painters in the house. They better stay away from you. *(He pulls her to him.)* You're my girl, Edna—

EDNA. Aw, Clancy—

CLANCY. You know it too, don't you? *(He kisses her.)*

MIDGE. *(Snaps picture.)* If I had a really good camera, I could enter a contest. *(Startled,* EDNA *and* CLANCY *turn.* MIDGE *smiles, pleased with self.)* Balcony seat—half price.

EDNA. *There,* Clancy!

CLANCY. Midge, did you—?

MIDGE. I did.

CLANCY. *(Starts up stairs)* We'll fix that.

MIDGE. *(Quickly opens door to her room)* Oh, I forgot to comb my hair. *(Dashes into room, slams door.)*

*(*CLANCY *is stumped. He cannot enter her room.* EDNA *laughs.* CLANCY *glares, descends stairs.)*

CLANCY. *(Grumbling)* I'd like to comb her hair with a rake.

MR. HARTMAN *(Off — upstairs — loud)* Doors slamming already! Who's that?

EDNA. *(*CLANCY *and* EDNA *exchange frightened glances)* Mr. Hartman, Clancy! Beat it.

*(*CLANCY *moves to sun parlor door.* EDNA *is suddenly very busy.)*

CLANCY. *(Under his breath)* The Hartman family!

MIDGE. *(Re-enters, without camera.)* Don't worry, Clancy. My lips are sealed. See no evil, hear no evil, do no evil.

EDNA. Doesn't sound like Midge.

MIDGE. *(Mock hurt)* Why, Edna—Not a word from Midge.

CLANCY. Good! See, Edna.

MIDGE. —Unless I want a favor sometime.

CLANCY. *(Stops short)* When you were ten, Midge, I always suspected you were a brat.

MIDGE. *(Mock shock)* Clancy—!

CLANCY. Now you're fifteen, I'm certain of it. *(Goes out Left 2)*

(MIDGE goes to table, takes muffin, eats.)

EDNA. Midge, why don't you just let life slide along on its own? Why do you want to be always messing in?
MIDGE. Tch, tch tch, Edna. "Messing in!" *(Goes to desk, muffin in mouth, scribbles a note.)*
MR. HARTMAN. *(Off—up—loud)* Cuff links, studs, old earrings—but could a man find *one* collar button?!
MIDGE. Oh—oh—Dad! *(Rises, goes to sun parlor door)* I'm off. *(Pauses at door).* What a day! Edna, isn't it great to be alive on days like this? *(Exits, with note)*
EDNA. A lot depends. Yes, siree, a *lot* depends.
(She is returning to dining room as MRS. HARTMAN descends stairs.)

(MRS. HARTMAN is a pleasant, tolerant, cheerful woman in her forties. She has a relish and appreciation for her children's charm, despite their often perplexing and irritating proximity. She enjoys trying to manage her home, children, and husband. At the moment she is dressed in a bright light dress which makes her look younger than her years.)

MRS. HARTMAN. Edna, did I hear Midge?
EDNA. You couldn't help it, Mrs. Hartman.
MRS. HARTMAN. Well, it's a real spring day! Is the coffee hot? Mr. Hartman's coming down now. *(Sniffs)* My, what an unpleasant odor.
EDNA. I'll get the coffee. I hope it doesn't taste like turpentine.
MRS. HARTMAN. Turpentine?

EDNA. They're painting today, remember?

MRS. HARTMAN. Oh. Well, do the best you can, Edna. It won't be a good day at best.

(EDNA goes into dining room as MR. HARTMAN comes down. He is a well-dressed, conservative business man. Even in his irritation and despite his temper, he is a charming man with much warmth in his personality. He puts his hat and coat on sofa, goes to card table, sits Left of it, opens paper, glances at headlines. MRS. HARTMAN rearranges table a bit.)

MR. HARTMAN. Confounded headlines! Takes your appetite away. *(Sniffs)* What's that?

MRS. HARTMAN. They're painting the dining room.

MR. HARTMAN. Good Lord, I forgot. This is the day for Virginia's guest—that refugee from a society column.

MRS. HARTMAN. This is the *week* for Virginia's guest, Jeff.

MR. HARTMAN. Week?!—Good Lord, I just remembered. Louise, do you know what we've allowed to sneak up on us again?

MRS. HARTMAN. What, Jeff?

MR. HARTMAN. Spring vacation again. The fatal week. *(Pages paper)* Why do you suppose an otherwise sane and responsible school board gives spring vacations? Next year I'm going fishing.

MRS. HARTMAN. That's what you say every year.

MR. HARTMAN. My sainted aunt! Here we are all over the society page. *(Sips orange juice.)*

MRS. HARTMAN. *(Looking over his shoulder)* So that's Carolyn Webster. Good looking girl.

MR. HARTMAN. Oh, I don't know. Virginia can hold more than a candle to that face, I'd say.

MRS. HARTMAN. Pride. Pure pride. *(Scans paper)*

"Will spend the week at the home of Virginia Hartman, daughter of—"—Oh, Jeff, they've misspelled your name. *(Sits Right of table.)*

(EDNA enters with coffee)

MR. HARTMAN. *(Obviously not liking it)* What does it matter? *(Taking out his suppressed irritation)* Don't we have coffee this morning?

EDNA. *(At his shoulder)* Good morning, Mr. Hartman. *(Looks up with an automatic smile, starts back to paper, sees a difference in EDNA.)* What are you all dressed up for?

EDNA. Miss Virginia's idea.

MR. HARTMAN. *(Surprised) Miss* Virginia?! *(Then he looks to MRS. HARTMAN)* Ten to one she wants me to dress for dinner.

EDNA. *(Withdrawing)* That Virginia sees all the movies.

MR. HARTMAN. They *all* see all the movies

MRS. HARTMAN. *(Returning paper to MR. HARTMAN)* Jeff, I think you forget that we were once in high school.

MR. HARTMAN. *(Buttering muffin)* Forget? Of course I don't forget. But we were normal, healthy children. As I remember it, we even studied once in a while—and we spoke English.

MRS. HARTMAN. They speak English—occasionally, and Elliott studies all the time.

MR. HARTMAN. Our son studies too darned much. The kid doesn't do anything else. No wonder his eyes are bad. I'd give five hundred dollars to see him go tearing out of here some day with a ball bat over his shoulder.—What about this book he says he's writing?

MRS. HARTMAN. Elliott keeps his own counsel these days. *(Whispers)* But between you and me, I think he's writing a great *tragedy*.

MR. HARTMAN. That's what I mean: it's *abnormal*. What does he know about tragedy? The only time he ever *looked* tragic was when he had the mumps.

MRS. HARTMAN. Well, he'll have to find those things out for himself. If we try to tell him, he'll make us the villains of the book.

MR. HARTMAN. I suppose it's normal, but did you ever look into those girls' closets? I opened Midge's closet the other day and five hundred movie magazines hit me in the face. And you should see what else—scrap books, broken toys, one-eyed dolls, rusty skates, and every old newspaper that's been delivered here in the past five years. *(MRS. HARTMAN is laughing)* Where the devil does she keep her *clothes?*

MRS. HARTMAN. Jeff, you're going to be late.

MR. HARTMAN. *(Disregards her)* A sense of responsibility—that's what I want them to have. *(VIRGINIA has entered and now stands on the landing. She is a slimly attractive young lady of the world, going on 18. Instead of her usual saddle shoes and skirt-and-sweater garb, she wears a trim suit, high-heeled shoes, and carries a perfectly matching handbag, gloves, and hat.)* When I was a boy—

VIRGINIA. *(With a detached air)* Oh, Dad, you can't instill repressions in the modern child. *(She comes down the steps, places accessories on table up Right and at the same time she looks in mirror and smooths her already smoothed hair.)*

MR. HARTMAN. Good morning, Virginia. *(To MRS. HARTMAN)* I thought if they didn't have to go to school they'd let us have breakfast alone this morning.

VIRGINIA. *(Ignoring him)* Keith will be here in ten minutes. He's going to drive me to the airport.

(MR. HARTMAN returns to paper)

MRS. HARTMAN. Hurry, Jeff—*(To* VIRGINIA*)*—I didn't know the Nolans were allowing Keith to drive their car during the day.

VIRGINIA. *(Drawing straight chair from rear wall down to upstage of breakfast table. Brightly:—)* Oh, they don't. He's driving ours.

MR. HARTMAN. *(Sputtering)* What! That kid wouldn't like to *buy* our car, would he?

MRS. HARTMAN. Jeff, you're going to be late.

VIRGINIA *(Tapping a glass with a fork as a signal for* EDNA*)* Of course, you know you should be grateful that I don't run around with every boy in town. I could, you know.

MR. HARTMAN. *(Dryly)* Yes, since you've more or less settled down to that rag-time Romeo, it seems less like a boy's gym class around here.

VIRGINIA *(To* MRS. HARTMAN*)* I know the painters are here, but how *long,* Mother, are we going to be eating in the parlor?—And oh, Father, don't call Keith a rag-time Romeo. The kids'll think you mean it.

MR. HARTMAN. I *do* mean it.

*(*VIRGINIA *shrugs)*

MRS. HARTMAN. I'm sorry about the parlor, Virginia. We'll be back to normal by lunch.

*(*EDNA *enters)*

VIRGINIA. I don't want to ask Carollyn to eat in the parlor.

MR. HARTMAN. From the looks of Carollyn, it won't matter where she eats. Your Mother and I were wondering whether she eats at all.

VIRGINIA. *(Ignoring him again. To* EDNA*)* Just one slice of toast, Edna, no crusts, and half a cup of weak tea.

EDNA. You in training?

VIRGINIA. Just because I don't gorge myself like my slap-happy sister — *(Remembering herself)* — please, Edna.

EDNA. My mistake. *(Goes into dining room.)*

VIRGINIA *(To* MRS. HARTMAN*)* You've never seen Carollyn. You have no right to talk like that.

*(*MR. HARTMAN *silently passes over the society page which* VIRGINIA *studies.* ELLIOTT *appears on the landing. He is just 16, tall, very slim, with hair that has rarely experienced a combing, wears a rather dour expression—an expression of detached intellectualism, an expression which he is rather determined to maintain. His eyes are those of a poet and he knows it. He wears unpressed tweed trousers, a very dark shirt and no tie.)*

VIRGINIA. Not a very good picture.

MRS. HARTMAN. Come down, Elliott. *(Rises, goes into dining room.)*

ELLIOTT. What an excellent odor.

MR. HARTMAN. *(Dryly)* Paint.

ELLIOTT. *(Suddenly)* Where?

MR. HARTMAN. The dining room.

ELLIOTT. The dining room! *(Dashes for dining room—the calm exterior utterly vanished.)* My typewriter, my notes, my books! If any ignorant painter has dared to touch my novel—

MR. HARTMAN. *(To* VIRGINIA*)* I suppose that's his artistic temperament coming out.

MRS. HARTMAN. *(Returns with cup, saucer, etc. She sets another place on table)* Elliott's upset again.

MIDGE. *(Enters from sun parlor)* How ya'all? *(During the following she goes to table, reaches over* VIRGINIA'S *shoulder, gets a muffin in one hand and a piece of toast in the other, goes behind desk,*

ACT I   AND CAME THE SPRING   21

Right, sits in chair with feet perched on desk.) Smell that spring in the air?

MR. HARTMAN. *(As before)* Paint.

MRS. HARTMAN. Where did you come from, Midge?

MIDGE *(With a gesture)* Darkest Africa, Mother. And there I met a black man who wouldn't say his prayers—I took him by the left leg—

VIRGINIA. Look at the way she's dressed!

MIDGE. Aw, can the sour grapes; this is spring vacation.

VIRGINIA. What will Carollyn think?

MIDGE. What do you want me to do, lace myself up in a corset?

MR. HARTMAN. Listen to that talk.

MIDGE. *Comfort* dictates *my* draperies. In India there's a tribe known as the comfort-dressers. They wear—

MRS. HARTMAN. *(Quickly)* Midge, did you clear out all those perfume bottles and movie magazines and did you take the signs off the walls?

MIDGE. All except the one that says "No dogs allowed". That Carollyn's just the kind of chicken to have a Pekinese.

VIRGINIA. I declare, Mother, if she talks like that, I'll be disgraced for life.

MRS. HARTMAN. Midge, you might try to fall back into English once in a whole.

MIDGE. Mother, your mind's been geared to the Nineteenth Century; you'll have to shift gears.

MR. HARTMAN. Nineteenth Century?!

MIDGE. Virginia, don't be so self-conscious. No wonder all my friends think you don't have any poise.

VIRGINIA. *(Highly insulted)* Don't have any—? Poise! That's very funny.

MIDGE. Thank you.

VIRGINIA. Your friends! That jitterbugging, loud crowd of—

MIDGE. Sister, sister — think of your lipstick. Think of your dignity. Think of the time you fell down in church.

VIRGINIA *(Appealing)* Mother, we simply *can't* have those infants, those imbecilic—

MIDGE. Are you referring to my friends, Gabby and Freddie?

VIRGINIA. We can't have them tearing around the place when Carollyn's here. It's indecent!

MRS. HARTMAN. Now, Virginia, they might get along very well.

VIRGINIA. Get along?!

MR. HARTMAN. *(A comment—very low)* Sounds like my office.

VIRGINIA. Mother, Carollyn goes to all the night clubs. They've taken her picture at the Stork Club.

MR. HARTMAN. I wonder where the modern man does go for peace?

MIDGE. When it comes to smart repartee, sister Ginny, depend on us.

(VIRGINIA starts to answer, decides against it, taps her foot, still seething.)

ELLIOTT *(Enters from dining room, somewhat pacified. He carries papers, books, etc.—places them on desk, his brow furrowed. Puzzled)* One of the painters was reading the *Main Currents of American Thought*. I wonder—do you suppose a man like that, a painter, could be interested in such a work? *(Sits on lower step, becomes engrossed in book.)*

MR. HARTMAN. *(Dryly—an explanation)* I'm paying them by the hour.

(EDNA returns, sets VIRGINIA'S breakfast before her.)

MRS. HARTMAN. Come eat breakfast, Elliott.
MIDGE. *(To EDNA)* I'm not very hungry, Edna.
EDNA. That sounds dangerous.
MIDGE. No hotcakes?
EDNA. No hotcakes.
MIDGE. Just cereal and bacon and eggs—two eggs.
EDNA. Elliott?
ELLIOTT. Huh?
EDNA. Breakfast?
ELLIOTT. Oh, why bother me? These trivialities always crop up to hinder and annihilate any great trains of thought.

(EDNA *turns and exits, her head high.*)

MIDGE. That's one of the themes of your book, isn't it?
ELLIOTT. *(Genuinely surprised)* How did you guess?

(MIDGE *smiles, waggles*)

MRS. HARTMAN. Are you watching your time, Jeff?

(ELLIOTT *goes for chair against rear wall.* MR. HARTMAN *does not answer*)

ELLIOTT. *(Seeing ALAN out front window)* Alan Fields approaches, Midge.
MIDGE. Don't tell me.

(MR. AND MRS. HARTMAN *exchange glances.*)

VIRGINIA. No, don't tell her. Imagine a sophomore snubbing a senior the way she does.

(KNOCK at Left 2 door)

MIDGE. Which comes first—your family or your class?

ELLIOTT. In Veblen's study of the modern conception of class—

(Another KNOCK)

MR. HARTMAN. *(Dryly)* Open the door, Elliott.

(ELLIOTT opens door. ALAN FIELDS is there. ALAN is 18. He has a shy, embarrassed manner which is at the same time winning and comic. In the course of the following scene he tries to keep his eyes off MIDGE, without much success.)

ALAN. *(Tentatively)* Hello—
MRS. HARTMAN. *(Going to door)* Come in, Alan.
ALAN. Sorry to interrupt. I mean—I don't want to—well, interrupt.
MR. HARTMAN. Not at all, Alan. How's your father?
ALAN. He's well. He's the reason I'm here.— Hello, Virginia!
VIRGINIA. Good morning.
ALAN. Elliott—
ELLIOTT. Hello!
ALAN. *(In a different voice)* Midge—
MIDGE. Isn't it a nice day? Yes, it's a nice day. Might be warm, though. (ALAN *shifts about.* OTHERS *regard* MIDGE *with varied expressions of astonishment and dismay.)* That exhausts the possibilities, Alan.
ALAN. *(Uncertainly)* Yes. Well, I'm afraid I don't quite understand all that.
MR. HARTMAN. Your father sent you?
ALAN. As a matter of fact, he did. He told me to tell you to call him this morning—some business deal or other.

MR. HARTMAN. *(Betraying excitement)* I'll do that! Yes, sir, it'll be a pleasure. Won't you have some breakfast, Alan?

ALAN. No, thanks. No. *(Pause)* Uh—nice day, isn't it? *(*MIDGE's *expression remains unchanged.* OTHERS *repress smiles.)* Wouldn't like to play tennis, would you, Midge?

MIDGE. Too warm, Alan.

ALAN. Warm?—Oh—They just opened the courts Saturday, you know. *(Pause)*—Well, so-long. Just wanted to deliver that message, Mr. Hartman. I'm working myself in the afternoons.

MRS. HARTMAN. *(Politely)* Are you, Alan?

ALAN. All afternoon. In a drug store. Not very pleasant work—

MIDGE. —So you play tennis in the morning.

ALAN. Uh—yes. *(At door)* Frisby's Drug Store. See you later. *(He smiles wanly and goes out door.)*

(Pause. Then the tensed family relaxes.)

VIRGINIA. That boy needs some lessons in chit-chat.

ELLIOTT. Ought to read more. Improves poise.

MIDGE. Lessons in dancing, too. And tennis. And sociability. And—just about everything under the sun!

MR. HARTMAN. *(Can stand no more—explodes)* That's a fine way to talk. You certainly make a man ashamed of his family. *(Rises—throws down paper. Even strides Left.)* Ashamed, get that! What's the matter with that boy?

VIRGINIA. Father, relax. *Please.*

ELLIOTT. Come, Dad.

MR. HARTMAN. Why, that boy's probably got as much intelligence, as many fine qualities—*more*— He's— *(Can't find word.)*

MIDGE. Dull's a good word. No color. No *savoire faire*.

MRS. HARTMAN. *(Coming to Right of table)* Jeff, finish your breakfast. *(Sits.)*

MR. HARTMAN. Well, he needs to be helped, not laughed at. I like him. And let me tell you something else: I like his father.

MIDGE. Oh, that's business.

MR. HARTMAN. Yes, it is. If Mr. Fields orders a fleet of trucks from me—a whole fleet, mind you—this extravagant family will be on easy street for a while.

MIDGE. Then I can get my camera—photo-flash and all.

ELLIOTT. Money, money, money!

MRS. HARTMAN. Sit down, Jeff. Alan's a very likeable boy. He always reminds me of Gary Cooper.

MIDGE. *(With a whoop)* Alan Fields in *The Lives of a Bengal Lancer.*

MR. HARTMAN. What have we done to deserve this? No sense of another's feelings, no normal, wholesome respect—

MRS. HARTMAN. Yes, dear. *(Picking up muffin and buttering it.)* But everyone must admit *Mrs.* Fields is dreadful.

VIRGINIA. Oh, you just say that because she's your rival in the garden club.

MR. HARTMAN. *(Subsiding into his chair again)* I give up.

(EDNA enters with breakfast for ELIOTT and MIDGE. ELLIOTT approaches his listlessly, bringing chair down below table; MIDGE, the opposite.)

MIDGE. *(To* MRS. HARTMAN*)* Sure! You walked off with all the prizes before Mrs. Fields' moved to town.

VIRGINIA *(To* MIDGE*)* But you *could* treat Alan better.

MIDGE. Of course! With tears in my eyes. My young heart is elsewhere.

VIRGINIA. I suppose you mean Buzz Lindsay. *(*MIDGE *waggles)* Well, don't be silly, that's all. *(Looks at watch)* Keith had better get here.

MIDGE. You don't care about Buzz. You and your Keith—that—acting snob—that—*ham*. Ever since he got the lead in the Senior Play, you've acted like a gazoon.

ELLIOTT. Love, love, love! It's all that's on your minds. If you would only come to the scientific realization that what you call love is merely a trivial emotion—chemical.

MR. HARTMAN. *(To* MRS. HARTMAN*)* There you are—not a normal one among the lot of them.

MRS. HARTMAN *(Smiling)* Don't be so sure, Jeff. It's spring.

ELLIOTT. That's a cheap cliché, if I ever heard one.

(EDNA, *shaking her head, exits Left 1.*)

MIDGE. *(Parking herself on desk)* Do you have *us* in your book, Elliott?

ELLIOTT. *(Rises and goes over to desk where he has placed his books and papers)* You? What could *possibly* be interesting about *you?*

MIDGE. I think I'm swell.

VIRGINIA. I hope Carollyn is broadminded.

MIDGE. Tolstoy! My own brother thinks he's Tolstoy!

ELLIOTT. Tolstoy! What do *you* know about Tolstoy?

MIDGE. *(Waggles)* Tolstoy and I are just like that. *(Holds up two fingers.)*

ELLIOTT. *(Figuring that an explanation is neces-*

sary now that attention has been drawn to him.) I really can't expect my family to understand, but my ideals of success are different from yours.

VIRGINIA. Hear, hear!

MRS. HARTMAN. Go on, Elliott.

ELLIOTT. Of course, I don't expect you to comprehend, but my ambition is higher than most ambitions. You see, I want to be a great success; if not in this life, at least in the life to come.

MRS. HARTMAN. You mean *heaven,* Elliott?

ELLIOTT *(Smiling tolerantly)* I mean posterity. I want my work to *live*. I want to be more than a *doctor* or a *salesman*.

MR. HARTMAN. *(Looks up sharply)* What's the matter with *selling?* *(Subsiding)* Besides, I'm manager of the sales department.

ELLIOTT. *(Books in his arm)* Fundamentally, nothing's the matter with it, but you'll have to admit, Father, that it doesn't contribute a great deal to posterity.

MR. HARTMAN. I've contributed three children to posterity.

ELLIOTT. *(Loftily, as he crosses toward sun parlor)* That's exactly my point. Unless *I'm* a success—*(Looks at his two sisters)*—you've contributed nothing. *(Exits into sun parlor.)*

MR. HARTMAN. *(Paper in hand, crosses to easy chair down Left)* If *I* would have spoken to *my* father like that—

VIRGINIA. Elliott has a right to his opinions. This is the Twentieth Century—*(Pause)*—But he makes me *sick*. *(Rises)*

(ELLIOTT *returns from sun parlor, crosses to dining room)*

MR. HARTMAN. Son—
ELLIOTT. *(Pauses above Left end of sofa.)* Yes?

Mr. Hartman. *(Gives up. He always finds it hard to say anything to his son with success.)* Oh, let it go.

Mrs. Hartman. Read your editorials, Jeff.—And watch your time.

(A WHISTLE is heard from porch beyond Left 2 door. Elliott, shrugging, goes into dining room.)

Virginia. If that's Buzz Lindsay, I'm not here. He never learned to knock at a door.

Midge. *(Eagerly, crossing to Left 2 door, throwing it open.)* Well, I'm here. *(Whistles shrilly.)*

(Mr. Hartman *winces.*)

Buzz. *(Off)* Hullo, kid! Your elegant sister around?

(Virginia *is crossing to stairs, pausing on lower steps with a regal air.*)

Midge. *(Disgusted)* She's here.

Buzz. *(Enters. He is* Virginia's *age, easy-going, casually dressed, interesting. To* All*)* Top of the morning.

Mr. Hartman. Hello, Buzz!

Mrs. Hartman. Glad to see you, Buzz.

Buzz. *(To* Virginia*)* I said top-of-the-morning, Ginny. (Virginia *takes two steps upstairs)* I mean —Virginia. (Virginia *pauses)* The milkman delivered your note. I didn't know you knew milkmen.

Midge. *(Hurriedly—tossing a muffin toward* Buzz, *who catches it.)* Have some breakfast, Buzz.

Virginia. Milkman? Note?—What's the gag?

Elliott. *(Enters from dining room, crossing to sun parlor, carrying a large, heavy typewriter.)* I don't see why *I* should be tossed around. — Hello, Buzz! *(Exits to sun parlor as* Buzz *waves, acknowledging greeting.)*

VIRGINIA. Will you tell me what is all this about a note?

BUZZ. *Your* note.

VIRGINIA. I haven't written you a note for months.

BUZZ. —Weeks. That's what's so funny about this one. But you shouldn't have placed the milk box in front of the screen door.

VIRGINIA. Buzz Lindsay, I haven't heard so much silly babble—

BUZZ. My father is a violent man, Virginia. There're two quarts of milk all over the front porch.

VIRGINIA. I certainly didn't write you any note, Mr. Lindsay—

BUZZ. —Telling me to hurry over here?

VIRGINIA. Telling you *anything!*

MR. HARTMAN. *(Looking at his watch)* Oh, great guns! Look at the time! *(Rises, rushes for coat.)* All this nonsense about a note. (MIDGE *giggles*) And what are you snickering about? (ELLIOTT *returns, crossing to dining room*) Salesman! And now I'm late. Why doesn't someone cooperate around this house! *(Hurriedly kisses* MRS. HARTMAN*)* Honey, if I can make this sale to Fields, we'll celebrate. *(Goes out Left 2.)*

(MRS. HARTMAN *closes door, leans against it.* OTHERS *smile.*)

MRS. HARTMAN. Every morning for twenty years. If it happened any other way, I'd be worried.

BUZZ. *(Gazing into* MRS. HARTMAN's *face) Now* I know what causes those lines.

MRS. HARTMAN. *(Laughing)* Silly!

BUZZ. And when I look at Virginia, I understand only too well. Oh, there was a girl.

VIRGINIA. Cut it, Buzz.
BUZZ. But something happened. What happened to Virginia?
MIDGE. She seceded.
BUZZ. No, child—she stuck to the Union but she gave Buzz the air.
MIDGE. Poor old Buzz!
BUZZ. Like an old shoe.
VIRGINIA. *(Airily, as she adjusts hat at mirror)* Think they're funny. Very witty twosome.
BUZZ. Come on, now, Virginia, you shouldn't sniff at a joke or two. After all—milkmen.
VIRGINIA. Buzz Lindsay, I did *not* send you a note. I wouldn't do such a childish thing.
BUZZ. You mean we're washed up, Virginia? Then I can call you Ginny the way I've always dreamed.

(There is a KNOCK at Left 2 door.)

MRS. HARTMAN. It's probably Keith. Now you young people behave. *(Goes upstairs.)*
MIDGE. We promise. (VIRGINIA *opens door.* KEITH NOLAN *is there. He is also* VIRGINIA'S *age—good looking, slender, well-dressed. His mannerisms and speech betray the fact that* KEITH *has ambitions of a theatrical nature. At the moment, expecting to be met by* VIRGINIA, *he is standing on porch, drawn up to his full height, more than a trifle stiff. There is a general pause while* ALL *survey him.)* It's Hamlet.
BUZZ. It's Lear.
VIRGINIA. *(To* KEITH*)* Come in, Keith. Right on time.
MIDGE. —It's that celebrated master of tragedy, Mickey-the-Mouse.
BUZZ. I was *never* on time.
VIRGINIA. We had breakfast in the parlor this morning. Isn't that silly?

KEITH. *(To* BUZZ*)* Hello, Lindsay. *(To* VIRGINIA*)*—When I was in New York last, I saw a Noel Coward play—they always had breakfast in the parlor.

(MRS. HARTMAN *enters on stairs, dressed for the garden — wide-brimmed hat, smock, etc., and pulling on gloves.)*

VIRGINIA. I thought it was very clever myself. But you know how parents are—so provincial.
MRS. HARTMAN. Aren't I the picture of the Provincial Lady?
KEITH. Good morning, Mrs. Hartman.
VIRGINIA. Here are the keys, Keith. *(Hands him keys.)*
MRS. HARTMAN. Try to dodge the street cars, Keith.
BUZZ. *(Confidentially to* MIDGE*)* I had a run-in with the police in Hotspur the other afternoon.
MIDGE. I heard.
MRS. HARTMAN. Speeding, Buzz?
BUZZ. That jalopy won't speed.
KEITH. *(Interested)* Why do you call it Hotspur?
BUZZ. Temperamental, full of anger. Cop said I was doing thirty, but Hotspur won't do more than twenty.
KEITH. Probably gave you a ticket for appearances.
BUZZ. No. It was a one-way street.
MRS. HARTMAN. *(Laughing)* Hurry back, Virginia. I'm eager to meet Miss Webster.
BUZZ. Aren't we all?—The milkman particularly.
VIRGINIA. *Will* you stop? For the last time—
KEITH. We'd better dash. Plane's due in ten minutes.
MIDGE. Did your father really trip, Buzz, on the milk box?

ACT I   AND CAME THE SPRING   33

VIRGINIA. *She* did it! Look at her face. *(They do)* Can't you tell? She forged my name just to get you over here!

MIDGE. Isn't that fantastic? *(Crosses to sofa.)*

MRS. HARTMAN. Midge, I don't like that.

BUZZ. I'll go right home.

MRS. HARTMAN. Midge, you'll have to learn—hands off other people's lives. Sometimes I think you're a very selfish girl. *(Goes into sun parlor.)*

VIRGINIA. Midge, I'll remember this.

BUZZ. For shame, Ginny. She put a lot of "X's" at the bottom.

(VIRGINIA, *unable to speak, stalks from room—out Left 2.* KEITH *follows.*)

KEITH. *(At door)* You're a very funny fellow, Lindsay.

BUZZ. They laughed when I sat down to play.

KEITH. Too bad you never learned any manners. *(Follows* VIRGINIA *off.)*

MIDGE. *(In the light bantering mood which she and* BUZZ *often share)* I had a manner once.

BUZZ. There are manners and manners. I'm developing a bedside manner myself.

MIDGE. Some day Virginia will throw her head in the air like that and it won't come down. *(Sits on sofa.)*

BUZZ. *(Sits on arm of sofa)* Come clean, Miss Hartman—why did you say—: "Please come. Vitally important. Soon. As ever, Virginia"?

MIDGE. Why did *I* say—?

BUZZ. 'Fess up, Midge. This is Buzz.

MIDGE. *(Deep in thought—serious)* Gosh, Buzz, you *do* know me, don't you?

BUZZ. Betcha.

MIDGE. That's why I wrote the note.

BUZZ. *(Puzzled)* The only trouble with you, Midge—is—you confuse a fellow.

MIDGE. Buzz, we're alike, aren't we?

BUZZ. Well—

MIDGE. We think alike. We laugh at the same things.—You look swell this morning, Buzz.

BUZZ. *(By now really uneasy)* Midge, you don't sound like yourself.

MIDGE. I'm tired of sounding like myself. I'm tired of *being* myself.

BUZZ. *(At a loss now)* Oh! *(To change subject)* Going to play tennis?

MIDGE. Yes.—No.—I don't know.

BUZZ. *(Rising)* Well—

MIDGE. Don't change the subject. Sit down.

BUZZ. *(Sitting on sofa)* Okay! *(Peering at* MIDGE*)* I'm a little busy this morning—looking for work.

MIDGE. *(Horrified)* You're going to *work* on vacation?

BUZZ. If I can find the work. Want to know a secret, Midge?

MIDGE. Is it a big secret?

BUZZ. For me it is.

MIDGE. *(Settling down—interested)* Shoot, Buzz.

BUZZ. You know, I've about decided to go into Medical School in the fall.

MIDGE. You like?

BUZZ. I like. But there's something else—something I've always wanted to do.

MIDGE. And—?

BUZZ. You'll laugh.

MIDGE. I might. Why not?

BUZZ. I think I'd like to play a clarinet.

MIDGE. You?—Music to soothe the common cold and make the appendix disappear.

BUZZ. Go ahead—laugh.

MIDGE. But I think that's swellelegant! Why don't you?

BUZZ. My Dad. He thinks it's silly.

MIDGE. Aren't parents absurd?

BUZZ. Do I laugh at him when he tells his tonsil story?

MIDGE. You should sometime.

BUZZ. —Or when he boasts he'll be elected Grand Master of the Masons?—Anyway, he squelched me the minute I mentioned this squeak-stick.

MIDGE. They run into money.

BUZZ. You know old man Barry's pawn shop?— (MIDGE *nods.*) He has one in the window. What a reed!

MIDGE. The question is—how much?

BUZZ. *(Rising. Pacing. Getting excited)* That's it! That's the unbelievable part of it — only fifteen bucks.

MIDGE. Only—!!

BUZZ. —Plus Hotspur for Mr. Barry's batty son.

MIDGE. You'd trade in your car?

BUZZ. I don't think it has any valves any more. And I know there's at least one spark plug missing.

MIDGE. *(Who has been thinking seriously, brow furrowed)* Buzz—

BUZZ. Yeah—?

MIDGE. We can get it.

BUZZ. *We?*

MIDGE. Sure! You and I. Oh, Buzz, I'm so glad you told me. You haven't mentioned it to Virginia?

BUZZ. Not yet.

MIDGE. *(Elated)* You told me first!

BUZZ. I better be on my way, kid.

MIDGE. Wait, Buzz. *(Intercepts his cross to door.)* Listen.—*(Leads him to sofa where they sit)* Listen —*(A bit breathless.)*

BUZZ. I'm listening.

MIDGE. Well, it's hard to say—hard for a *girl* to

say. (Buzz, *uneasy again, starts to rise.* Midge *takes his hand, draws him down.*) When a girl reaches a certain age—no, that won't do. (Buzz's *expression shows that he would like to help—but he doesn't know what to say.*) Well, things happen to her. Not ordinary things, either. Big things. *(Desperately)* Take any girl—any average girl, for instance—and she finds a boy—not just *any* boy— (Buzz *again tries to rise—he looks very uncomfortable*) And she knows if she lives to be a hundred—or two hundred—

Buzz. *(Trying to pass it off)* She can't do that.

Midge. Don't do that—don't *joke*.

Buzz. Sorry, Midge.

Midge. Well, look at it this way. *(Goes to table, takes a cream pitcher and a coffee cup and holds them up.)* Here's a girl *(the cup)* and here's a boy *(the pitcher).* *(Arranges these on floor, then reaches to table for another cup which she exhibits.* Buzz *watches, puzzled, interested, but honestly embarrassed.)* Now this is another girl — older maybe. Suppose the boy prefers this girl—or *thinks* he does. Really he doesn't know, but he *thinks* he does. *(Looks up, bright-eyed.)*

Buzz. It gets rather complicated.

Midge. It *is* complicated. Or it used to be. *(Picks up first cup)* The whole world says this girl can't say anything to this boy—about her—*feelings*—but this is the Twentieth Century—we're *modern*, aren't we?

Buzz. *(Uncertainly)* Sure!

Midge. And minds can be changed. People *do* change. You don't just go on caring for a person if that isn't the person for you.

Buzz. *(Again trying to pass it off with a laugh)* In Africa they say you change if it snows. Of course, it never snows.

Midge. Please stop that silly joking.

Buzz. Midge, listen—you're too young to—

Midge. Young! Young!! *(Crashes cup to floor.)* Well, I'll get your clarinet for you—and I won't laugh—and that's more than any of your *old* people can do!! *(She dashes, near tears, flushed and angry, into the sun parlor.)*

(A pause. Buzz scratches his head, looks after her. He stoops and gathers up parts of the cup on the floor. Elliott enters from dining room.)

Elliott. Now what new imbecility—?

Buzz. *(Looking up, grins)* Mice, I think.

Elliott. One interruption after another! What's that? *(Indicates pieces of cup.)*

Buzz. That's Midge. Or it might be me; I don't remember.

Elliott. *(With a scornful look)* Don't bother explaining. Whoever it is, it sure dropped a bomb into Chapter Thirteen.

Buzz. *(Depositing pieces on table)* This book you're writing, Elliott—is it *funny?* Is it a comedy?

Elliott. A comedy? Funny? What's *funny* about life?

Buzz. A lot of things. Elliott, why don't you come out and play a little baseball? Give you a whole new viewpoint.

Elliott. Please don't be ridiculous. In the first place, I don't *need* a new viewpoint and in the second place, I know of nothing more useless than batting a little ball around a field. *(His final and conclusive judgment on the subject.)*

Buzz. Well, it's always fun coming over here. My family's on the dull side. One sister knits, the other plays bridge.

Elliott. Your father's a doctor. That must be dramatic, full of interest.

Buzz. Dad's got a touch of rheumatism. Makes

him blind to other things. But you can always depend on it here—a whirlwind, a tornado, or at least a cyclone.

ELLIOTT. I'd give ten years of my life for a little peace and quiet. I wonder whether Milton had a family.

BUZZ. So-long, Elliott. If it begins to look too tough in the book, look around you. You might get a laugh out of things.

ELLIOTT. You wouldn't say that if you lived here. So-long. (BUZZ *goes out Left 2.* ELLIOTT *lounges on sofa, his eyes on the ceiling, hands clasped behind his head. He is the picture of repose. After a moment, the PHONE jangles loudly.* ELLIOTT *jumps to a sitting position. Bitterly, as he crosses to phone)* Alexander Graham Bell!

(Before he can reach for phone, MIDGE *dashes in Right, crosses quickly to desk, picks up phone just as* ELLIOTT *is reaching out his hand. She smiles across mouthpiece.)*

MIDGE. This is Midge. (ELLIOTT *throws up his hands, returns to sit. Head in hands, thinking.*) Yes, Dad— She's in the garden— Mr. Fields is going to buy the trucks— What trucks?— Okay, I'll tell her— No, Virginia hasn't come back yet— (ELLIOTT *goes into sun parlor*) —No, don't hang up, Dad. I want you—I want to tell you something. Well, I thought with this Carollyn Webster coming and all, *something* should be done about the car— it's sort of dirty and it needs shining—or even simonizing. And I know just the person—Buzz Lindsay! (ELLIOTT *returns with a very thick book open in his hands. He is reading obliviously. Sits center during the following.*) He'll do it very reasonably— He needs— (*Her face brightens at what she hears; then the pleased expression falls into one of terror and desperation.)* No, Daddy! *No! (Utterly dejected)* I didn't mean that *at all. (Wails)* Please, Daddy. *(Slumps)* Just a moment. *(Then to* ELLIOTT, *in a small voice.)* He wants to talk with you.

ELLIOTT. *(Reluctant)* Me?—That's odd. *(Goes to phone.)* Hello! (MIDGE *goes to sofa, picks up book, tries to read.)* Yes. *(Brightly, unsuspicious)* Oh, I feel fine— Of course I get enough exercise— *What!? (Repeating his father's words)* When I get *married!* But you know I have no intention of ever getting married, Father. I have my life all planned and worked out. Marriage means shrieking and messiness and squalling children, — not for me— You mean *washed?* Simonized! ! ! *(Glares at* MIDGE *who looks up furtively, gestures helplessly.* ELLIOTT *speaks evenly, tense, and angry.)* Yes— Yes— I understand. *(Replaces phone; starts for* MIDGE *with murder in his eyes.)*

MIDGE. *(Rises, backs away)* Elliott, I didn't mean you at all. I meant Buzz.

ELLIOTT. It'll be *good* for me, he says. "Good for me!"—Simonizing that whole sedan car!

MIDGE. He'll pay you, Elliott. You can use the money for your encyclopedia fund. He said he'd pay you.

(All the while ELLIOTT *has backed her around sofa up to stairs.* MIDGE *is poised, ready to run.)*

ELLIOTT. He told me again that he was captain of his basketball team and Phi Beta Kappa at the same time. Balance, he said. *Balance!*

MIDGE. It won't take long, Elliott.

ELLIOTT. Just one day! Just one whole afternoon away from my book!

MIDGE. Look at it philosophically, Elliott.

ELLIOTT. *(Pausing—drawing himself up)* You are

right. One mustn't be jolted into a loss of perspective.

MIDGE. *(Agreeing)* One mustn't indeed!

ELLIOTT. *(Developing his line of thought)* But the sooner people around this house realize I am *not* a man of action, the better. *(Stalks up the stairs)* The next time, try to stop and think, Midge. Consider the wasted effort in polishing a car—rubbing, shining. *(Looks down at* MIDGE*)* You and your brilliant mind! Next to the collected works of Plato you'd be the perfect companion on a desert island. *(Goes off upstairs.)*

MIDGE. Why, thank you, brother dear. *(Crosses to Left 2 door, opens it, as* CAROLLYN WEBSTER, VIRGINIA, *and* KEITH *enter, loaded with airplane luggage.* CAROLLYN WEBSTER, *at 17, is trying hard to live up to her publicity. She wears a smartly tailored travel suit, a huge cartwheel hat, high heels, and a pretty, attractive—but still-life—expression. Her long hair falls down the side of her face in the fashion of the times. Around her neck, hanging on a shiny strap, is a leather-encased, very expensive candid camera.* MIDGE, *meeting them at the door, is momentarily embarrassed. She quickly recovers, throwing the door fully open for them.)* Oh!—*Entrez-vous*. Take off your hats and shoes. This is Shangri-La.

VIRGINIA *(Entering)* Come in, Carollyn. And don't mind her. My sister, Midge, and she's apt to seem a little strange at first.

CAROLLYN. I've heard so much about you.

MIDGE. I've seen your picture somewhere. Smooth, smooth— You were never mixed up in a scandal, were you?

CAROLLYN. Not yet, sorry.

MIDGE. I read all the tabloids I can get hold of. I've seen that face.

VIRGINIA. Cut it, Midge.

MIDGE. And what a camera! A beauty!
CAROLLYN. Thank you. *(Flashes a bewildered look to* VIRGINIA.*)*
KEITH. Well, I'll be trotting along now.
CAROLLYN. *(Extending her hand)* You've been a big help. (KEITH *takes her hand.)* And we've become such *frightful* good friends, haven't we?— In such a *dreadfully* short time.
KEITH. Oh, we'll get better acquainted. *Much* better, I hope.
CAROLLYN. We must. But *positively*. We have so much in common. *(Turns to* VIRGINIA*)* Don't you think so, Virginia?
VIRGINIA. *(Coldly)* I couldn't say, I'm sure.
KEITH. *(Struck by her tone. Moves to Left 2 door)* Well—well—*au revoir*.
CAROLLYN. And thanks again.

(KEITH *goes, smiling at* CAROLLYN.*)*

MIDGE. *(With feigned sudden inspiration)* I remember now! You're the girl who's to be our house guest. Of *course*. —How do you do, Miss Webster?
ELLIOTT. *(Upstairs)* Midge! Midge!— When Virginia gets back with that giggling, simpering female, let me know.
MIDGE. *(Enjoying* VIRGINIA'S *embarrassment—calling)* I shall, Elliott. *(Smiles to* CAROLLYN*)* Our brother, Elliott. A very nice character.
ELLIOTT. *(Continuing—off)* —Though why I should have to suffer—varnishing a car—just because my sapheaded sister wants to impress a—
VIRGINIA *(Calling)* Elliott!
ELLIOTT *(Continuing)*—flat-faced glamour girl who probably reads dime novels in dollar covers.
MIDGE. You suffer, Elliott.
VIRGINIA. *(To* CAROLLYN—*not convincingly)*

He's joking. He's a great kidder. He knows we're here, so he's joking.

MRS. HARTMAN. *(Entering from sun parlor)* How-do-you-do? You're Carollyn. Welcome to our little town!

CAROLLYN. *(Uncertain now)* Mrs. Hartman, it was so sweet of you to ask me.

MRS. HARTMAN. We're happy to have you. You'll find us very informal here.

CAROLLYN. *(With a meaningful glance upstairs)* I know.

MIDGE. Oh, Virginia—

VIRGINIA. I'll show you your room, Carollyn.

MIDGE. Ginny, want to do me a favor?

VIRGINIA. *(For* CAROLLYN's *benefit)* Why, of course, Midge.

(CAROLLYN *and* MRS. HARTMAN *chat together upstage.*)

MIDGE. Lend me fifteen dollars, Virginia.

VIRGINIA. What?!

(Both CAROLLYN *and* MRS. HARTMAN *look up at sound of voice.)*

MIDGE. Fifteen dollars. It's of vital importance, really.

VIRGINIA. You're being funny. *(Sotto)* This is no time to talk about money.

MIDGE. —If you don't have it, I have a terrible job cut out for myself.

VIRGINIA. *(Under her breath)* You be careful. I'll talk to Dad if you act like this all week.

MIDGE. Do you realize how badly I *need* a mere fifteen dollars?

VIRGINIA. *(Turning away—speaks to* CAROLLYN*)* Ready, Carollyn?

CAROLLYN. Of course! *(They start up the stairs as* ELLIOTT, *attired in too-large mechanic's coveralls, comes downstairs, carrying a handful of rags.* CAROLLYN, *who precedes* VIRGINIA, *comes face to face with* ELLIOTT *on the stairs. Interested, she says:)* I'm Carollyn.

ELLIOTT. I'm the garage man. You look just the way I expected you to look.

CAROLLYN. Thank you.

ELLIOTT. That's no compliment. *(Brushes by her and down the stairs.)*

MRS. HARTMAN. *(Sharply)* Elliott!

VIRGINIA. Really, that's the rudest—

CAROLLYN. How quaint!   *(WARN Curtain.)*

MRS. HARTMAN. Elliott, will you carry Miss Webster's bags upstairs for her?

ELLIOTT. Sure— Sure— I'm dressed for it.

MRS. HARTMAN. What are you doing in that preposterous costume?

ELLIOTT. *(Bag in hand)* Me?— I'm waxing the car—after I do this errand. I don't have anything to do during vacation. *(Starts upstairs.)*

(CAROLLYN, *seeing him coming, goes with* VIRGINIA *following, and* ELLIOTT *bringing up the rear.)*

CAROLLYN. Virginia, what a fascinating family! So indi*vid*ual!

VIRGINIA. *(Very weakly)* They're not always like this, really. It must be—spring or the weather or something.

CAROLLYN. *(Off now)* Unusual!

ELLIOTT. *(Disappearing)* My book's not important. It can wait. What's a great novel to America?!

MIDGE. Elliott thinks he's Ernest Hemingway!

MRS. HARTMAN. *(After casting many doubtful looks after the trio upstairs, jerks around at men-*

tion of Hemingway.) Midge, you haven't been reading—! !

MIDGE. That defeatist—not me! I'm going to *get* what I want—so watch my dust! *(Goes into sun parlor.)*

(MRS. HARTMAN *looks after her.* ELLIOTT *comes stamping down steps.)*

ELLIOTT. Magnificent Midge—the miracle-maker! *(Goes out into sun parlor as* MRS. HARTMAN *watches. With an expression of apprehension and growing dismay,* MRS. HARTMAN *sinks into Center chair—a picture of fear as*

THE CURTAIN FALLS

ACT TWO

Scene I

Scene: *Same.*

Time: *Tuesday, immediately after dinner.*

At Rise: *The lamps are lighted, giving a pleasant glow to the room and it is dark outside. The breakfast table has disappeared. SOUNDS of laughter, voices, and the general commotion of the evening meal come from the dining room. After a slight pause, the dining room door opens and* Midge, *wearing bright skirt and sweater, emerges. SOUNDS louder when door opens.* Midge *crosses to desk, picks up neatly folded evening paper. With a stealthy glance toward dining room, she opens it, pages furiously, finds what she wants, drops paper to floor and sprawls on top of it in her eagerness.*

Midge. "Help Wanted—Female. Help Wanted—Male." *(She scans hurriedly)* "Baker, bootblack—" *(Shaking head—mumbles along)* "—Horse trainer!" M-m-m, horse trainer. *(Considers this, decides against it, mumbles along to—)* "Window washer. Experienced." *(Face lights up.)* "Tenth Floor." *(Anger)* Tenth-floor! Not for Buzz. *(Rests her head on hands, thoughts far away.)* Buzz. *(Jolts her-*

self out of her study, reaches for paper, proceeds to tear the want-ad page into parts, saving some, discarding others.)

(MR. AND MRS. HARTMAN *enter from the dining room. SOUNDS rise—*ELLIOTT, CAROLLYN, VIRGINIA;*—an argument is evidently developing. * MR. HARTMAN *is shaking his head.* MRS. HARTMAN'S *smile is broadening into a half-laugh. By this time* MIDGE *has worked herself into position just Right of chair Center, concealed from* MR. *and* MRS. HARTMAN.)

MR. HARTMAN. *(Sitting on sofa, not noticing paper which is now spread across floor pretty generally.)* The Tariff—what do they know about the Tariff?

MRS. HARTMAN. They studied it one week in school, Jeff—and it was the debate subject last year. *(Sits on Left arm of sofa.)*

MR. HARTMAN. Politics, Taxes, the Tariff, the Supreme Court! Will you tell me why three growing youngsters should want to sit through supper arguing— *(The VOICES in dining room rise.)*—There, listen to that!

MRS. HARTMAN. They just don't agree with *you,* that's all, Jeff.

(During the above, MIDGE, *unseen by* MR. *or* MRS. HARTMAN, *crawls on hands and knees upstage Center, rises at stairs. She is now stealthily ascending.)*

MR. HARTMAN. That is *not* all! Now they're arguing modern art — surrealism — impressionism — hands sticking up in the middle of a desert that looks like an ocean but is really just someone's imagination! That constant chatter with the smell of paint doesn't agree with my gastric juices, Louise.

MRS. HARTMAN. Maybe we should feed them before we eat; that's the way we used to do, remember?

MR. HARTMAN. And why must they garble that horrible corkscrew language? One minute they sound like some ancient tribe of barbarians and the next they talk in that darned Oxford English. Confuses a man.

MRS. HARTMAN. *(Sinking onto sofa next to him)* After all these years, do you still ask for consistency, Jeff?

MR. HARTMAN. *(Filling pipe)* And I can't say I like their *condescending* to me all the time, either. I lace my own shoes.

MRS. HARTMAN. *(Laughing)* You don't expect to know as much as they do, do you? They've lived hundreds of years.

MR. HARTMAN. Do you know what I wish, Louise?— I wish all of them were just three or four years old, and I wish they'd stay that age—past the diaper stage but still no psychoses. Do you realize these modern kids are a whole new race?

MRS. HARTMAN. Don't fool yourself, Jeff. That's just what our parents thought. I have a feeling that these young people are just exactly the way we were—inside. I imagine they were always the same.

MR. HARTMAN. You mean *I* was once like that?

MRS. HARTMAN. Very much, Jeff.

MR. HARTMAN. I never was.

MRS. HARTMAN. You—and I—and the Greeks—and Romans—and the cave dwellers—and the Indians, I suspect—and the Chinese—all the way down the line, in all ages.

MR. HARTMAN. But somewhere children have respect for their parents, at least, don't they? *That* didn't go out with the bustle, did it?

MRS. HARTMAN. I don't think there's any disrespect attached, Jeff. It's just a new way of talking and acting. A lot of things changed with the bustle.

Mr. Hartman. Louise, when I was a boy—

Mrs. Hartman. *(Slipping her arm through his)* Jeff, did you ever notice the expressions on their faces when you tell them about the time you were captain of the team and Phi Beta Kappa at the same time?

Mr. Hartman. Well, I *was* captain and Phi Beta Kappa at the same time.

Mrs. Hartman. I know, dear, but think how you felt when your father told you he crossed the mountains laying railroad ties, working his way.

Mr. Hartman. *(Remembering, speaks impulsively)* Oh, he got so confounded *tiresome*— *(Breaks off—guiltily)* —Say, are you trying to trap me?

Mrs. Hartman. *(Laughing)* Let them growl at us for a while and we'll smile at them—and growl a bit too—and in a few years they'll have families of their own. And they'll understand what we meant and their children will growl at them. They may express themselves differently, Jeff—but the same old feelings are there underneath.

Mr. Hartman. *(In search of matches, rises and crosses to desk, stumbling over the paper spread on the floor)* Now what? *(Looks at date on paper)* This is *tonight's* paper! We'll soon know who tore it out. If it's the beauty hints, it's Virginia; if it's recipes or garden notes— *(Looks up.)*

Mrs. Hartman. Honestly, Jeff, *I* haven't seen the paper.

Mr. Hartman. Neither have I— That's what I mean. If it's the book section, it's Elliott. *(Fumbling and examining paper as he talks)* And if it's the movies or sports, it's Midge— *(Looks up, infinite surprise on his face)* Good Lord, it's the help wanted ads!

Mrs. Hartman. Then it's no one in *this* family.

ACT II　　AND CAME THE SPRING

(MIDGE *comes down the stairs breezily.* MR. HARTMAN *turns to her.*)

MIDGE. Dad, if I were to try to explain something to you, you wouldn't be heartless, would you?

MR. HARTMAN. First I want you to answer me a question. Why don't we have the paper sent to the house in the evening?

MIDGE. Because you get it at the office.

MR. HARTMAN. And why do I get it at the office?

MIDGE. *(Innocently)* So you can read it—before it's been—clipped.

MR. HARTMAN. Now answer me truthfully, Midge— Did you or did you not utterly destroy this newspaper?

MIDGE. Utterly destroy?—Now, Dad, we're getting off on the wrong foot—

MR. HARTMAN. Answer yes or no.

MIDGE. *(Crestfallen)* Yes.

MR. HARTMAN. *(Pause. He regards her, then quickly he steps across and places his two hands on her arms, shakes her gently and then huskily)* Thanks for telling the truth! *(Goes to Left 2 door, picking up his hat as he goes)* I'm going out to get a paper. *(Goes out, closing door.)*

MIDGE. *(In a small voice)* I would have gone.

MRS. HARTMAN. *(Picking up the rest of the paper and stuffing it into the waste basket)* Midge, I wonder what it will take to make you picture consequences. *(Shakes head)* Now, what was it you didn't want your father to be heartless about?

MIDGE. *(Changing mood)* It's like this—suppose there was a fellow and a girl—no—last time I broke a cup— (MRS. HARTMAN *looks up quizzically.*) Fifteen dollars suddenly seems like a lot of money, Mother.

MRS. HARTMAN. Fifteen dollars *is* a lot of money.

MIDGE. Not for a gobstick when you put Hotspur with it.

MRS. HARTMAN. *(More and more confused)* You don't want to start at the beginning, do you?

MIDGE. I just did— Look, Mother, there's not a thing in the want ads that even remotely pertains— And I have the dress and all—and Saturday night means a good deal to me—a great good deal, Mother—

MRS. HARTMAN. *(Gently)* Has he asked you, Midge?

MIDGE. *(Slowly)* Well—no. Not yet, I mean. Don't you see—that's why it's so important.

MRS. HARTMAN. Important?

MIDGE. For me to be able to do a little favor for him like this—so he'll realize—so the darn fool will realize! There ought to be some way a girl can raise fifteen dollars!

(The dining room door opens again and ELLIOTT, CAROLLYN and VIRGINIA enter. ELLIOTT is talking to CAROLLYN.)

ELLIOTT. That's not an idea, that's a *vaudeville* joke.

VIRGINIA. *(To CAROLLYN)* Isn't he the *rudest* thing?—It gives him personality, though.

CAROLLYN. *(To MRS. HARTMAN)* Your son is the most extra*ord*inary person. He's *bursting* with ideas, and if there's *anything* the world's short on, it's ideas.

ELLIOTT. *(Going into sun parlor)* You *read* that somewhere.

MIDGE. *(Flopping into chair—down Left)* I never got to finish a conversation in my life.

CAROLLYN. *(To VIRGINIA)* Did you say you played ping-pong? Why, I haven't played ping-pong for years.

ACT II AND CAME THE SPRING 51

VIRGINIA. Would you like to play?

(TYPEWRITER has been going in sun parlor.)

MRS. HARTMAN. Elliott is—
VIRGINIA. Elliott's been in the sun parlor all day; let him move; we want to play ping-pong. Come on, Carollyn.
CAROLLYN. Why, I hope I'm not disturbing anything.
VIRGINIA. Of course not.

(They are gone off Right.)

MRS. HARTMAN. *(Going to table up Right, getting hat)* Well, got to dash. Midge, tell your father I've gone to the Arrangement Committee meeting—for the Flower Show.
MIDGE. *(Resignedly)* Okay!

(MRS. HARTMAN *puts on hat and gloves; goes to Left 2 door. As she opens it we hear* BUZZ'S *whistle and she goes out. Their VOICES are heard off. Meanwhile* MIDGE *dashes to mirror over table, fluffs her hair, straightens skirt.* BUZZ, *dressed very much as before, enters. Pause.* MIDGE *and* BUZZ *survey each other,* BOTH *more than a trifle embarrassed. Before either speaks, the sun parlor door is opened and* ELLIOTT, *carrying typewriter, enters, crossing toward dining room.)*

BUZZ. Do you write on that thing, or just carry it around?
ELLIOTT. *(Shaking head)* Women, Buzz, women!
MIDGE. We're not so bad.
BUZZ. *(Smiling)* Midge, you're just a kid.

(ELLIOTT *goes into dining room.*)

MIDGE. *(Quietly indignant)* Please stop saying that, Buzz.

BUZZ. Okay! You're an old lady with nice freckles and a long white beard.—Where's Virginia?

MIDGE. Oh, around— Buzz—

BUZZ. Yeah, Midge?

MIDGE. Drag up a breath and sit down, won't you?

BUZZ. Sure!

(BUZZ *sits on Right end of sofa.* MIDGE *on chair Center.*)

MIDGE. *(Abruptly)* Just how modern are you, Buzz?

BUZZ. *(Half-rising)* Now why do you want to start all that—

MIDGE. *(Halts him with gesture)* Don't worry, I won't get tangled up this time. I've thought about it enough, all Heaven knows.—Buzz, if you're half the person I think you are, you'll look at this thing right.

BUZZ. Look, Midge—

MIDGE. Now don't take to the woods.—Who are you taking to the Prom Saturday night?

BUZZ. As a matter of fact, that's why I'm here—

MIDGE. *(Exalted)* You *are?*

BUZZ. *(Uneasily—but gently)* To ask Virginia.

MIDGE. Oh— Face the facts, Buzz.

BUZZ. I always try.

MIDGE. Don't you see it? Doesn't it stand out all over her?—Virginia's gone on Keith. Completely gone! You and I—we have such fun, don't we?

BUZZ. We do, Midge— You're pretty frank, kid.

MIDGE. Honesty is our motto. We aim to please. —And you should see my dress—Buzz, you've never seen me in an evening gown.

Buzz. No.

Midge. You couldn't've. This is my first. It has a hood.

Buzz. Midge, you're sweet.

Midge. *(Elated)* Then you will?!

Buzz. I didn't say that.

(KNOCK at the Left 2 door.)

Midge. *(Reluctantly rising—groans)* Someone interrupts every conversation I've *ever* had.

Buzz. Open it, Midge.

Midge. *(Crosses to door)* We'll return to our discussion anon. *(She opens door.)*

(Christine Myers *enters—or rather, tears into the room.* Christine *is 17, dynamic, athletic, dressed roughly. She is school cheer-leader as well as captain of about every girls' athletic activity. She is the kind of a girl who, as cheer leader, somehow shakes a spectator's confidence in a team of mere boys. She walks with head jutting out in front, shoulders hunched over.)*

Christine. Hello, Midge! Hiya, Buzz! *(Before either can answer she breezes on)* Where's Virginia? —Say, Midge, you're pale. Do you think you get enough exercise? (Midge *starts to answer*) Get out in the sun more. Nothing like the sun to give a girl vitamins and confidence! Old Man Sol! Am I right, Lindsay?

Buzz. You should know, Christine.

Christine. I *do* know. Look at me. Do you find me sitting around Bradley's Barbecue all day and all night? Well, where's Virginia? Got some club business to discuss.

Midge. She's playing ping-pong.

Christine. *(Outraged)* Ping-pong! Do you mean

to stand there and tell me that a healthy girl in high school would waste time playing ping-pong? Midge, your sister is a natural-born high-jumper.

MIDGE. *(Going to sun parlor, opening doors)* You better tell her yourself, Christine. She'd think I was kidding.—And I would be, too. *(Exits.)*

(Even BUZZ is a bit uneasy with the overwhelming CHRISTINE.)

CHRISTINE. Well, Buzz, old man, how's it go with you?

BUZZ. Oh, fine! And you?

CHRISTINE. Fine, fine!—Except for my studies. I have a time with mathematics and botany.

BUZZ. Too bad.

CHRISTINE. But I'm going to teach Physical Education—don't need much book stuff for that.

(VIRGINIA enters from sun parlor. BUZZ rises. CHRISTINE turns.)

VIRGINIA. Hello, there, Christine!—Why, Buzz, I didn't know you were here.

BUZZ. Surprise, surprise!

CHRISTINE. Virginia, you don't look well. You don't look well at all.

VIRGINIA. *(Smiling)* I never do. Sit down, won't you?

CHRISTINE. Can't stay. Got to run. Got to get to bed—getting late. *(Brings out envelope)* Here, Virginia—these are the funds for the club pins. Pat Carrington had to go out of town over vacation and you've been elected official treasurer for the sub-deb club—*pro* something or other.

VIRGINIA. *Pro tem.* Very well, Christine. But why aren't we getting our pins before the dance?

CHRISTINE. As I understand it, we need six

more— *(Looks at* Buzz*)* —Is it all right to talk in front of him?

VIRGINIA. Of course!

CHRISTINE. Well, we only need six more dollars— that's one new member—or no pins. In the meantime, you hang onto the money— Well, got to go now.

BUZZ. Sleep tight.

CHRISTINE. I will, Lindsay. I *always* sleep tight. So-long, Virginia.

VIRGINIA. Good night. Light enough for you out there?

CHRISTINE. *(On porch)* Smell the air—spring! Bye! *(She is gone.)*

BUZZ. Do you suppose she ever *walks* anywhere?

VIRGINIA. She's off at a dead run. *(Smiles)* You should see her throw the javelin.

BUZZ. No, thanks.

MIDGE. *(Enters from sun parlor)* Has the Amazon gone?

BUZZ. Tell me, Virginia: when do sub-debs come out?

VIRGINIA. Don't try to be funny.

BUZZ. I'm not, honestly.—When do sub-debs become debs, if ever?

VIRGINIA. *(Crosses to dining room, opens door, calls)* Elliott!

(BUZZ *looks to* MIDGE. *Shrugs.* MIDGE *smiles.* ELLIOTT'S *TYPEWRITER ceases.)*

BUZZ. Where's this new razzle dazzle from points east?

VIRGINIA. So *that's* what you came for?

ELLIOTT. *(Off)* I'm busy.

VIRGINIA. Come here just a few minutes, Elliott. Important. *(To* BUZZ*)* She's in there. I want you to meet her. (ELLIOTT *enters, leans against dining room* *door frame.)* Oh, Elliott—Carollyn's waiting for you to play with her.

ELLIOTT. *(Betraying interest)* Me?

VIRGINIA. Be a good chappie and don't insult her this time.

BUZZ. *(Echoing)* "Chappie"?

ELLIOTT. *(Half protesting, but strolling across toward sun parlor with a definite interest, running hand through hair)* Nobody realizes how important my book— Oh, well, what's ten minutes? *(He exits.)*

VIRGINIA. Buzz, I want to talk to you— *(Looking at* MIDGE*)* —alone. *(She comes Left of sofa and stands facing him.)*

(BUZZ *doesn't rise.)*

MIDGE. I'm not going anywhere if that's what you mean.

VIRGINIA. *(Giving her an ignoring glance)* Buzz, do you have a date for the dance?

BUZZ. What!! }
MIDGE. What!! } *(Together)*

VIRGINIA. *(Hurriedly)* Because if you haven't, I know the most charming girl—

BUZZ. *(With a glance toward sun parlor)* Oh! There for a minute I thought I'd made a conquest.

MIDGE. What did I tell you, Buzz? She'd palm you off to any female Tom, Dick or Harry.

VIRGINIA. I'm talking to Buzz, Midge. No children allowed.

MIDGE. Virginia, I hope you're passing through a stage. You are potentially a very unpleasant person.

BUZZ. *(To* VIRGINIA*)* To tell you the truth, Countess, I came to ask *you* to the Prom.

VIRGINIA. Oh, but I've got a date—or at least I *think* I have.

MIDGE. She means he hasn't asked her yet. I know what she means when she talks like that.

ACT II AND CAME THE SPRING 57

VIRGINIA. *(Shooting* MIDGE *a dark, ignoring glance)* Come on out and meet her, Buzz, and then you'll *want* to go with her. I know you will.

MIDGE. Take a gander, Buzz, and if she doesn't nauseate you, I'm disappointed.

BUZZ. Okay!. *(Rises)* No harm in looking.

(VIRGINIA *and* BUZZ *go into sun parlor.* MIDGE *looks after them a moment, undecided, and reaches for her trusty phone.)*

MIDGE. *(Into phone)* Ridgeway 5436. *(Drums with fingers)* Hello! May I speak with Keith?— Keith, this is Midge—well, don't *sound* like that. I'm going to do you a favor— You know who's here now —Buzz Lindsay, and he's trying to date your sweet dish, so shake the lead, Romeo, before it's too late— *(With infinite sweetness)* That's all ri-i-ght.

(Before she hangs up there is a CLATTER on the porch, the door Left 2 opens and MR. HARTMAN *with his newspaper,* GABBY ALLEN *and* FREDDIE NORTH *burst into the room.* GABBY *and* FREDDIE *are an energetic 15. They are dressed brightly, speak their own language and are most uncomfortable when still.)*

FREDDIE. Look what we found. *(Jerking a thumb at* MR. HARTMAN*)* He looked so sad we decided to pep him up.

MIDGE. *Gabby!*

GABBY. *Midge!*

(They greet each other like college alumni in the middle of a desert. MR. HARTMAN *makes for the stairway.)*

FREDDIE. Not off for the shuteye? *(To* MR. HARTMAN*)* The moon just popped.

GABBY. Ain't your father on the beam?

MR. HARTMAN. No, Gabriel, I'm not on the beam. *(Goes up)* Midge, has your mother gone?

MIDGE. About ten minutes ago.

MR. HARTMAN. Hm-m. Now if the telephone, by some accident of fate, *should* be for me, I'll take it upstairs. *(Exits upstairs.)*

MIDGE. Sure, Dad. Sleep tight.

FREDDIE. *(Coming down into room)* Gee, ain't that the way all fathers are? Always *one* valve missing?

GABBY. *(In a whisper)* Where is she?

MIDGE. *(Jerking her thumb to sun parlor)* Ping-pong.

FREDDIE. What variety shemale is she?

MIDGE. *(Burlesquing it)* Hair down to here, my deah. And *so* chic, chic, chic! And I told you she flew— *(Waves arms)* —and listen,—

GABBY. (FREDDIE *and* GABBY *gather closer)* I'm all ears, nose, and throats.

MIDGE. She's built like a totem pole. *(Gestures her hands in two straight lines.)*

GABBY. On the level?

FREDDIE. I've seen those streamlined powder-puffs before.

MIDGE. And she oozes glamour—but synthetic.

FREDDIE. When do we get a squint?

MIDGE. I'll take you out now, but act blasé, for Pete's sake.

GABBY. I guess Virginia's all of a doodah.

MIDGE. Ready to collapse.

(FREDDIE *goes to radio, turns it on, and soon loud swing music fills the room.)*

MIDGE. —But I got something really world-shaking to ask you. You two are still doing the same dance, aren't you?

FREDDIE. Just a little static once in a while, but we're solid. *(Smiles at* GABBY, *who grins.)*

MIDGE. Well, I don't know how to say it, but—
GABBY. *(Eagerly)* Yeah—?
MIDGE. But I think it's—well, it's hit me at last.
GABBY. No!? Ah, Midge!
MIDGE. I feel funny all the time and especially this week I've felt—peculiar.
GABBY. Freddie, come're.
FREDDIE. *(Doing a dance—returns)* What's on the fire?
GABBY. It's Midge—she's been hit—
FREDDIE. Gosh, you mean—?
GABBY. A bolt of lightning.—Who is it, Midge?
MIDGE. I've known him all my life and—
GABBY. I know: it's been slowly growing all that time. Who is it?
MIDGE. Buzz Lindsay.
FREDDY. *(With a gesture)* That intellectual!
MIDGE. It's insufferable, but there you are. *(Drops into chair Center.)*
GABBY. Can we do anything, Midge?
MIDGE. Maybe. *(Thinks)* Maybe you can. After all we're old enough—and the world's old enough—to know that love isn't just something that happens—like a weed.
GABBY. That's right.
MIDGE. It's more like a flower. You have to plant it—and care for it—and—well, love is something you *do* something about. Am I right?
GABBY. Perfectly. } *(Together)*
FREDDIE. Absotively. }
MIDGE. Look—Virginia goes for Keith, which is silly—but typical. And—well, Buzz *thinks* he likes Virginia.
GABBY. "Thinks"?
MIDGE. Well, no one like Buzz could *really* like Virginia, could they?
GABBY. I guess you're right. *(Sits heavily on sofa. Shakes head.)* We'll help, won't we, Freddie? (FRED-

DIE *nods.*) But it'll take method. Tons of method.

ELLIOTT. *(Storms into room)* She's a cad!—What does *she* know about Omar Khayyam? I write better when I'm mad, anyway! *(Goes into dining room and slams door.)*

GABBY. Isn't he medieval?

FREDDIE. *(Rising abruptly)* Well, let's go greet the glamour girl.

MIDGE. Remember what I said—blasé.

(They exit to sun parlor.)

MR. HARTMAN. *(Comes downstairs, his face red with anger)* Midge! Virginia!—This thing has simply got to—— *(Looks up, sees room is empty, irascibly crosses to radio, viciously turns off music. Goes back upstairs mumbling)* They're never here when they ought to be here.

(VIRGINIA *enters from sun parlor with* BUZZ.)

BUZZ. She's not a very good ping-pong player.

VIRGINIA. *(Turning to him)* Well?—

BUZZ. I had my mind set on you, Virginia.

KEITH. *(Knocks at Left 2 door and enters. Crossing to* VIRGINIA, *taking both her hands)* Bon soir, Virginia! *(Turning to* BUZZ, *tone changing)* Hello, Lindsay! *(Back to* VIRGINIA*)* How's every little thing?

BUZZ. How are the actors these days?

KEITH. We're all right. How are the country quacks?

BUZZ. Tops.

VIRGINIA. *(Shows surprise, interest and some resentment)* I didn't know you'd decided on anything, Buzz.

BUZZ. *(Crossing to chair down Left—sitting)* Entering Med School in the fall. Then I'll probably come right back here.

VIRGINIA. You mean you want to live here all your life?

BUZZ. Well, people get sick here, too. And I guess if everybody wanted to get off to a big city, the cities would just get bigger and dirtier and pretty soon—no towns like this.

KEITH. That would certainly suit me.

BUZZ. And I like towns like this myself.

KEITH. Once I saw New York, I knew. There's a city! Real things doing—activity—life—lights.— What do you say, Virginia? Which would you like?

VIRGINIA. Of course, I'd like to *see* New York. But— *(Enter CAROLLYN from sun parlor. VIRGINIA rises.)* There you are, Carollyn. How did you find the children?

CAROLLYN. Quaint.

VIRGINIA. Keith and I were just going out to play —besides, Buzz wants to talk to you.

BUZZ. *(Protesting)* No, I—

KEITH. Buzz, why don't you go on out with Virginia? We'll join you when we finish the conversation we started yesterday—right, Carollyn?

CAROLLYN. *(Draping herself on sofa)* That should be exquisite.

VIRGINIA. *(Haughtily, turning on BUZZ)* Buzz Lindsay, don't you *ever* do anything right? *(Storms into sun parlor.)*

(BUZZ, *scratching his head, smiles, follows. Alone with* CAROLLYN, KEITH *assumes his most sophisticated air. He is consciously going into a love scene which he attempts to carry off with the aplomb of one of his favorite stage characters.* CAROLLYN *is looking at* KEITH *with veiled expectancy.)*

KEITH. It's been an eternity since we talked.
CAROLLYN. Only yesterday.
KEITH. *(Crossing down to desk, placing fingers of right hand on it, speaking his line with his back to CAROLLYN)* Still, it *has* been a long time.
CAROLLYN. Quite!
KEITH. *(Trying to get up momentum)* Quite! *(Pause,—he is stymied. Turning to CAROLLYN and leaning nonchalantly against desk.)* You know, of course, that there's some ridiculous dance on Saturday night?
CAROLLYN. *(With a rising inflection)* Yes?
KEITH. *(Brittle)* Of course, you can't expect these provincial affairs to be as exciting as what you're used to—the theatre, the Rainbow Room, The Stork—
CAROLLYN. *(Sweetly)* Oh, but I believe one should adapt, don't you?
KEITH. Yes, but it's a little hard to adapt to the gym when you're thinking of the Waldorf-Astoria. *(Then suddenly)* Don't you think Noel Coward writes the most fascinating plays?
CAROLLYN. Aren't they unbelievable!? Brittle?
KEITH. Quite!
CAROLLYN. Absolutely brittle!
KEITH. I knew you'd think so. *(Returns and sits in chair Center, crossing his legs—a man of the world.)* We seem to have a lot in common.
CARROLLYN. Undoubtedly. I think it's wonderful to exchange opinions and—*things* about plays and music and niteries and *things*.
KEITH. *(Rising; sitting next to CAROLLYN on the sofa)* If we went to the silly old dance, we wouldn't have to dance much, you know—and be bumped into by all those jitterbugs and all.
CAROLLYN. Aren't they a scream? I honestly think they're the most screamingly mad people I've ever watched.

KEITH. Then say you'll go and maybe it won't be so boring this time. *(Puts his hands over* CAROLLYN'S.*)*

CAROLLYN. But you impulsive boy. Haven't you invited someone else already?

KEITH. *(Becoming less brittle)* Well, I haven't exactly invited—that is, it's come up in conversations but we sort of—brushed around it.

CAROLLYN. But you wouldn't want to take *me*. I'll be the stranger—and anyway, you'll want to go with a *beautiful* girl.

KEITH. You're beautiful. *(Takes her shoulders in his hands.)* With your hair and those eyes—

CAROLLYN. Keith!

(The dining room door opens and, unseen, ELLIOTT *enters.* KEITH *is just about to kiss* CAROLLYN *when* ELLIOTT *speaks.)*

ELLIOTT. Carollyn, is he bothering you?

(CAROLLYN *and* KEITH *arise abruptly.)*

KEITH. You stay out of this, Elliott. Go write a poem.

ELLIOTT. Carrollyn, if he's insulting you—

KEITH. I'm not insulting her, and what would *you* do about it?

ELLIOTT. Well, I'd do the only thing—a gentleman —*could* do about it.

KEITH. *(His sophistication completely escaping him)* Go hire an army.

CAROLLYN. *(Pleased)* Now, boys, this is utterly, utterly—

KEITH. *(Regaining some of his composure)* Of course you wouldn't know how to carry off a scene like this.

ELLIOTT. I'll carry *you* off! You can't come into my house and insult my visitor!

KEITH. *(Thoroughly angry) Your* visitor!?

CAROLLYN. Isn't this exciting?

ELLIOTT. *(Removing glasses)* I suppose it will be necessary—

KEITH. This is childish.

ELLIOTT. You call me childish!?—You silkworm poseur.

KEITH. By golly, if you want to fight—

CAROLLYN. *(Rising)* Boys, boys, I will *not* have you fighting about me.

ELLIOTT. If he insulted you—

KEITH. If you don't stop *saying* that—

CAROLLYN. Keith—ple-e-ease—

KEITH. *(On his dignity again)* Very well, Carollyn. If that's the way you want it. *(Goes to* CAROLLYN, *takes her hand and bends over as though to kiss it.)*

ELLIOTT. *(Thoroughly enraged)* What are you going to do? (KEITH *glances at* ELLIOTT *over his shoulder, shrugs, smiles at* CAROLLYN *and goes to Left 2 door.* ELLIOTT *turning away, unable to watch)* The things a man has to contend with.

KEITH. And Carollyn, I wont take "no" for an answer. *(Exits Left 2.)*

(CAROLLYN *crosses to* ELLIOTT, *who now stands at the foot of the stairs, drumming his fingers on the newel post.)*

CAROLLYN. *(Softly)* Elliott, you would have fought with him?

ELLIOTT. *(In a smothered tone)* Maybe I would have.

CAROLLYN. I've never known *any*one that gallant.—You're angry at me.

ELLIOTT. *(Stiffly)* I'm not angry.

CAROLLYN. I always thought that authors and writers—and—you know—*things*—I always thought they had to control their tempers— I suppose you have a *lot* of girl friends, Elliott?

ELLIOTT. *(Turning to her, very conscious of her nearness)* Not many. A man in my position, with things to say and things to do, can't really afford much time— *(His voice trails off—)* I like your hair down the side of your face like that.

CAROLLYN. Why, Elliott, that's the sweetest thing. *(Turns down Left and sits on Left arm of sofa while she speaks.)* I don't want you to tell me how beautiful I am. Anybody can make up nice things about your hair.

ELLIOTT. *(Following her and leaning across back of sofa)* I'm not making it up. *(Stiffly)* —But I see what you mean.

COROLLYN. You were so angry with me before.

ELLIOTT. I was angry at your ideas. But I have thought it over. You don't know what a relief it is to meet a girl who has *any* ideas.

CAROLLYN. Oh, *my* head's not filled with moonlight. That's what the doctor said when I was psychoanalyzed.

ELLIOTT. *(Impressed)* You've been psychoanalyzed?

CAROLLYN. And the doctor said I shouldn't try to be too intelligent—after all, I was very beautiful.

ELLIOTT. I—think—so—too.

(ELLIOTT *is leaning very close to her and she is slowly turning to him as the sun parlor doors burst open and* VIRGINIA, *followed by* BUZZ, *enters.)*

VIRGINIA. Those fleabrains—ping-pong's one thing and jitterbugging is another—and they don't mix.

Buzz. *(Smiling)* Calm yourself. I think it was pretty funny.

Virginia. *(Whirling on him)* You would—you honestly would. You think *everything* is funny. (Buzz *shrugs, goes to sit in chair behind desk. Meanwhile* Elliott *and* Carollyn *spring apart and* Elliott, *with an exclamation of disgust, has crossed to Left 2 door. He pushes it open and stands looking out moodily.)* Where's Keith?

Carollyn. Well—

Elliott. I kicked him out.

Buzz. *(Laughing)* You what!?
Virginia. *(Astounded)* What!? *(Together)*

Elliott. He got fresh, so I kicked him out.

Virginia. Well, really—of all the impolite—Well!—Carollyn, we're going to Bradley's Barbecue for a coke-and-sandwich.

Carollyn. What's that?

Buzz. Just a little joint with a juke-box.

Carollyn. How quaint!

Virginia. *(Back on her high horse)* Shall we freshen up? *(Exits upstairs.)*

Carollyn. *(Crossing to* Buzz *and smiling across the desk)* Do you play golf, Mr. Lindsay?

Buzz. A little.

Elliott. *(Coming down behind* Carollyn*)* I play golf. When do you want to play?

Carollyn. *(Turning to* Elliott*)* Why, Elliott, exquisite! *(Smiling brightly at* Both *of them, runs lightly upstairs and off.)*

(Left alone with Buzz, Elliott *is a bit embarrassed. He stands undecided for a moment and looks after* Carollyn.*)*

Buzz. Since when do you play golf, fella?

Elliott. I've got to learn. *(Leans eagerly across desk)* You can't tell her, Buzz.

Buzz. Who's telling anybody?

Elliott. Will you teach me?

Buzz. Well, it takes more than a day. I'll do what I can.

Elliott. *(Uncertain and crossing slowly down to Center, stands with back to chair)* Buzz—

Buzz. Uh-huh?

Elliott. Can you dance?

Buzz. I can't teach you *that*.

Elliott. I've got to learn by Saturday.

Buzz. Get your sister's friends. They know a hundred dances I never heard of. They make me feel like a creaky old man. *(Looking up.)* You got a date for the Prom?

Elliott. I will have.

Buzz. Virginia's got her heart set on my taking the Duchess.

Elliott. Who?

Buzz. You know—Carollyn Whosis. Got a hunch I might do it. I'm not sure whether Virginia gives a hang for me or not, but she's got a jealous streak.

Elliott. This love business would drive a sane man to a padded cell! You haven't asked her yet?

Buzz. Not yet.

Elliott. You haven't got a chance. *(Turning suddenly)* What about fighting, Buzz?

Buzz. Fighting?

Elliott. Sure, you know. *(He takes an exaggerated Nineteenth Century boxing pose—fists upturned, body stiff)* I read a book once.

Buzz. That was a pretty old book, wasn't it?

(PHONE rings. And as usual, Midge bursts into room from sun parlor, grabs phone, smiles at Buzz.)

Midge. This is Midge. (Buzz *crosses to* Elliott) —Well, who *do* you want?— *(Disappointment)* Oh!

Buzz. *(To* Elliott*)* Don't lift your hands so high. *(Shows* Elliott *how to hold hands for fighting.)*

Midge. *(Laying down phone, going to foot of stairs)* Dad, telephone!

Elliott. *(Resuming old pose)* In the book it said—

Mr. Hartman. *(Off)* I'll take it up here, Midge. Please hang up.

Buzz. *(Tapping* Elliott *lightly in the stomach with his left hand)* No protection. Bend over at the belt.

(During the ensuing conversation, Midge *hangs up phone and, as before, walks several steps away but finds the temptation too great. Returns to phone, holding hand over mouthpiece—listens intently.)*

Elliott. *(Bending over at the waist at a stiff angle)* Like this?

(At this point Gabby *and* Freddie *enter from sun parlor. They are doing the Conga,* Freddie *behind* Gabby.*)*

Freddie *and* Gabby. *(Together)* One, two, three, bump— (Gabby *catches sight of* Buzz *and* Elliott *in fighting poses, cries)* Fight!!! *(They rush over.)* Give him the old one-two!

Freddie. *(Excited)* Muss up his face—you gotta use footwork.

Mr. Hartman. *(Off—loud)* Has the circus come to town?

*(*Virginia *and* Carollyn *come running downstairs.)*

VIRGINIA. Elliott, what's gotten into you?
FREDDIE. Elliott has turned into a mauler.
BUZZ. *(Laughing, putting his arm around ELLIOTT)* Come on, Elliott. Buy you a barbecue.
ELLIOTT. They won't mind, will they—my going to that place?
MIDGE. *(Still on phone)* Shh!
CAROLLYN. This is the nicest house—so much—*life.*
FREDDIE. *(Singing)* We're off to see the Wizard—the wonderful Wizard of Oz.
GABBY. *(Linking her arm through ELLIOTT'S)* Come on, Elliott. Let's hot foot it down to the Barbecue and cut a rug.
ELLIOTT. *(Stiffly, as he goes out Left 2 with FREDDIE and GABBY)* Very well. Coming, Carollyn?
MIDGE. *(Slamming phone on hook) Wait!* Buzz, I've got it!
BUZZ. Got what?
VIRGINIA. *(To CAROLLYN)* What you must think! Coming, Buzz?
MIDGE. Wait—he can't now. Buzz, stay here a minute.
VIRGINIA. Well, Buzz, if you prefer children—
CAROLLYN. I'll save you a place, Mr. Lindsay.

(VIRGINIA *and* CAROLLYN *go out Left 2.* MIDGE *runs to* BUZZ; *stops within a few feet of him.*)

BUZZ. *(Calling after them)* You can pile in Hotspur—I'll drive you over. Don't tear your skirts when you climb over the door. *(Then back to* MIDGE*)* Well?—
MIDGE. Buzz, it's dropped into our laps.
BUZZ. What has?
MIDGE. The whole plum tree—the whole solution! Now you can get your clarinet.
BUZZ. I don't see—

Midge. You know who that was on the phone?—Mr. Fields.

Buzz. Alan's father?

Midge. The same. First he talked a lot of silly business and *then*—he asked Dad whether we could spare our gardener to help Mrs. Fields, and Dad said yes because of this deal that's on.

Buzz. Following.

Midge. Don't you see—*you* can be our gardener. Just go over to Mrs. Fields and say—"I'm Mrs. Hartman's gardener."

Buzz. But isn't Mrs. Fields the woman who wants to take some prizes away from your mother?

Midge. Isn't it ghastly—her gardener just up and quit—but it's pluperfect! This is Tuesday. By the end of the week you'll be able to get your gobstick.

Buzz. And who's going to hide your real gardener for the week? Besides, I know *Alan* Fields.

Midge. *(Stopped momentarily)* Oh! *(Thinks—brightens)* Well, Alan works. He told me so himself—all afternoon.

Buzz. And what about the gardener—Clancy?

Midge. I've got it!

Buzz. What?

Midge. Clancy and Edna—I've got a picture that cinches it—cinches it beautifully!

Buzz. A picture?

Midge. Blackmail—a little healthy blackmail. I'll take care of Clancy—I'll make him go fishing. *(Auto HORN sounds.)* Oh, Buzz, look—we've done it. I'll take care of the whole thing myself. All you have to do is pull a few weeds.—Buzz, isn't it marvelous? *(In her enthusiasm, she takes his arms in her hands.)*

Buzz. I hope you know what you're getting into, little lady.

Midge. *(Intensely)* Don't you see—don't you see, you blind fool—I'd do anything for you, Buzz.

AND CAME THE SPRING

(Before Buzz can move she leans over and kisses him lightly on the lips. Then she links her arm through his and leads him to Left 2 door.)

Buzz. Midge, you crazy—
Midge. *(Hushed)* Please don't talk, Buzz. Just go on off to Bradley's.

(Auto HORN again.)

Buzz. Aren't you coming?
Midge. Not tonight. You go on along—and be sure to be at Mrs. Fields' house first thing tomorrow afternoon. *(Straightens his tie and pushes him out the door with infinite gentleness. She closes door, leans against it. Sound of CAR. Midge crosses slowly to sofa, sinks down, lying on back. She stares dreamily at ceiling.)* So this is what they mean.
Mrs. Hartman. *(Enters Left 2; starts upstairs—catches sight of Midge. Quietly)* Hello, Midge!
Midge. *(Dreamily)* Hullo!
Mrs. Hartman. Anything wrong, Midge?
(WARN Curtain.)
Midge. Wrong?—Not a thing in this world. *(Pause)* I wonder, though—do other people—I mean —did *anyone* ever feel like this before?
Mrs. Hartman. I imagine so. *(Smiling. She comes down and turns off lamp up Right. LIGHTS dim.)* Yes, I rather think so—cave dwellers and Indians and Chinese and Victorians.
Midge. Mother, I don't get all that.
Mrs. Hartman. Never mind.—You don't have to talk about it unless you want to, dear.
Midge. But I would like to— (Mrs. Hartman *goes Center, her eyes full of understanding.)* —Yet I don't—or can't. Gosh!—Gosh, I feel all hard and soft and tight—at the same time. And *new*—not like the same person at all. *(Pause)* Good night, Mother.

Mrs. Hartman. *(Turns off lamp Center. LIGHTS dim.)* Good night, dear. If you want to talk later, come into my room. *(Goes to stairs; starts up.)*

Midge. *(Sits up)* Fate— (Mrs. Hartman *pauses on stairs*) That's part of it! Mother, do you believe in Fate?

Mrs. Hartman. *(Trying not to smile—really touched)* I must confess I haven't thought about it for—some time.

Midge. I know modern science eschews the idea. —But what if I'd been born in some other town. I could have gone through my whole life without feeling this. *(Breaks off—half to herself)* How can anything be so wonderful and so terrible at the same time? *(Then embarrassed, with a hasty abashed glance at her mother)* I don't mean—I know I'm only sixteen—almost—but maybe young people are older younger nowadays. (Mrs. Hartman *raises her brows.* Midge *goes to Left 2 door; throws off all LIGHTS at wall switch; opens door. MOONLIGHT floods in.*) I think I'll sit on the porch for a while—by myself. The way I feel, I'm almost afraid —of something. (Mrs. Hartman *starts to speak, catches herself—decides against it.* Midge *looks up.*) It's a wonderful night. Feels like summer. *(Goes out door into blue light.)*

(Mrs. Hartman *is looking after her—from dimness—with mixed emotions as*

THE CURTAIN FALLS

ACT TWO

Scene II

Scene: *Same.*

Time: *About ten o'clock, Wednesday evening.*

At Rise: Clancy, *in football jersey, sits in Center chair, looking downcast and uneasy.* Freddie *is perched on back of sofa with feet in same. The RADIO is blaring and* Gabby *is improvising dance steps down Left.* Gabby *and* Freddie *are dressed in their casual, bright, characteristic manner.* Midge, *wearing slacks and sweater, is sitting Indian fashion on the desk. The room is cheerfully lit and bright moonlight streams through the window and Left 2 door when it is opened.*

Clancy. But I don't *like* fishing.
Freddie. I never heard of anybody who didn't like fishing.
Clancy. Well, I thought I would. I tried to like it. I thought— Clancy, what a break! You get paid for working all afternoon and all you have to do is sit there and hold a pole.
Midge. Well?
Clancy. Well, I held a pole. And I went on holding it. I held it till my arm was so stiff I can't scratch my neck where the mosquitoes got me—and nothing happened. Nothing.—No, sir, I'd rather work.
Midge. Work!
Freddie. Work!
Gabby. Nuts in the beard.
Clancy. But why? Why should I fish all after-

noon, keep my mouth shut, and still collect my regular salary?

MIDGE. It's only for a week, Clancy.—You have to stay out of sight.

FREDDIE. And we thought the best way was to go fishing.

MIDGE. Of course, if you'd rather take a bus over to Badgerville or some place.

CLANCY. But why do you fresh kids *want* me to do all this?

GABBY. "Fresh"?

MIDGE. *(Seriously quoting)* "Yours is not to reason why, yours is but to do and die."

GABBY. *(Improvising dance steps, dramatically)* "Into the jaws of death, into the mouth of hell, rode"—a lot of people.

CLANCY. Nope. I think I'd rather work. I don't see how anyone in his right senses could prefer fishing to working.

FREDDIE. My father does.

GABBY. *(Resignedly)* Show him the picture, Midge.

MIDGE. I hate to resort to such methods, Clancy. *(Reaching into pocket, pulling out photographs. As though dealing cards,* MIDGE *makes a neat display of the snapshots around her.)* Mother and Dad, Virginia swimming, me, me, me, me, me. *(With each word she lays down a picture)* Elliott shining the car, Buzz, Buzz, Buzz, Buzz, Buzz,— *(In the same tone)* Gabby and Tommy—

FREDDIE. Gabby and who!?

GABBY. *(Stops her dance abruptly, her hands still in the air)* What!?

MIDGE. *(Blithely, with a wink to* GABBY*)* Did I say Gabby? I meant Flabby and Tommy.

FREDDIE. *(Crossing to her determinedly)* Give us a gander.

MIDGE. *(Concealing photo)* It doesn't concern you, Mr. North. What would Flabby say?
FREDDIE. Who's Flabby?
MIDGE. The girl that goes with Tommy.
FREDDIE. You said Gabby.
GABBY. *(To MIDGE)* I wouldn't have dreamed it of you! My best friend. Why, we've been pals from the cradle!
MIDGE. We're still pals. This isn't your picture.
FREDDIE. *(Turning on GABBY)* What would you be doing with that Tommy Litchfield?
GABBY. She didn't say it was Tommy Litchfield. And besides she said it was Flabby.

(All through this little scene CLANCY has been jerking his head from one speaker to the next. Finally:—)

CLANCY. Now I *am* mixed up.
MIDGE. *(Finding the picture she wants)* Here it is. Clamp your peepers on this, Clancy.
CLANCY. *(Looking at picture, speaks dolefully)* You snapped it, all right.
MIDGE. Monday morning, remember?
CLANCY. Don't Edna look cute?
GABBY. *(Ignoring FREDDIE, with complete nonchalance, the "Tommy" subject is closed—she crosses to look at picture over CLANCY's shoulder)* Is it incriminating? *(Sees picture)* Clancy, you look like a movie star.
CLANCY. *(Pleased)* Do I?
GABBY. In a western. They hire a lotta football players.
MIDGE. Where did you learn to kiss like that, Clancy? You've even got your eyes closed.
CLANCY. *(His face lights up)* I got it! *(He tears up picture and jams it in his pocket.)* *Now* you won't show it to Mr. Hartman!

MIDGE. Got a negative and four other prints.

FREDDIE. *(Who has crossed to chair down Left and is now sitting with his chin on his two fists, gazing dolefully into space)* Tommy Litchfield of all people!

GABBY. *(With a look at MIDGE)* I guess I know who my friends are.

MIDGE. Can the static, you two. *(Crosses to FREDDIE)* This was years ago.

FREDDIE. *(Rising)* Then it *was* Gabby?!

MIDGE. *(Exasperatedly)* It was *Flabby!*

CLANCY. *(Moving to outside door)* Well, I'll go home now, and I'll go fishing tomorrow afternoon, but I won't like it—all by myself.—You might tell me where I'm *supposed* to be.

MIDGE. *(Going to him)* Are all football players so dim? You're supposed to be at Mrs. Fields', tending her garden, but Buzz is doing it.

CLANCY. *(Bewildered)* Now it gets worse. Maybe I just better not know. *(Looks at the three)* But you're building up to an awful let-down. *(Scratches head.)* I wish I could think faster. *(He goes out Left 2.)*

MIDGE. 'Night, Clancy.

FREDDIE. *Anybody* but Tommy Litchfield!

(PHONE rings. MIDGE answers as usual.)

MIDGE. This is Midge— *(To GABBY, referring to radio)* Cut the barrelhouse.

(GABBY, understanding, flips off radio.)

FREDDIE. If it's my Mother, tell her she was right about Gabby.

GABBY. Oh, *your* Mother—!

MIDGE. Who?—Yes, Mrs. Allen, Gabriel's here.

ACT II AND CAME THE SPRING 77

(Offers the phone to GABBY*)* Gabby, it's Scotland Yard.

FREDDIE. Tell her I'm bringing you right home.

MIDGE. *(Crosses to Center table, picks up* CAROLLYN'S *candid camera which has been lying there from the beginning of the scene, crosses to* FREDDIE *in an attempt to be friendly)* Have you seen this camera, Freddie?

GABBY. *(On phone)* But, Mother, this is vacation.

FREDDIE. *(To* MIDGE*)* Don't talk to me about cameras.

GABBY. *(In phone)* —But it's only ten o'clock, the middle of the afternoon.

MIDGE. *(Fondling camera)* It's Carollyn's but I'm going to have one. *(She slings it over her shoulder, adjusting it with care.)*

GABBY. *(On phone—patiently)* I am *not* a *growing girl.*—And we've just swung into action.

(MIDGE *aims camera at* FREDDIE.)

FREDDIE. *(Violently)* Stay away from me. You and your blackmail and your cameras!

MIDGE. *(Lets camera drop with a jerk on her neck)* Freddie!

GABBY. *(Into phone)* You always have the advantage. I'll come home, and I'll go to bed, but don't expect me to go to sleep for *hours.*

FREDDIE. *(At door, stiffly)* Come, Miss Allen.— Tommy Litchfield! *(Goes.)*

GABBY. *(Replaces phone; goes to* MIDGE*)* I never thought I'd see the day, Midge Hartman. Your big bazoo has probably wrecked my life. *(Goes.)*

(MIDGE, *crushed, goes to radio, flips it on. A "blues" number fills the air.* MIDGE *replaces camera on Center table and helplessly sits in chair Center as* ELLIOTT *enters from dining room.* ELLIOTT *is dressed as before except that now a pipe protrudes almost challengingly from between his lips, not necessarily lighted.)*

ELLIOTT. Are the—uh—others back yet?

MIDGE. *(Sadly)* Carollyn's not back yet. *(Looks up; sees pipe.)* Does Carollyn like pipe-smokers?

ELLIOTT. *(Regarding pipe ruefully)* I've used four boxes of matches. It won't stay lit. *(He returns to dining room.)*

(MIDGE *rises, leaves the radio on, turns down LIGHT and goes upstairs. After a moment* MR. *and* MRS. HARTMAN *enter from Left 2 door.* MR. HARTMAN *is speaking as they enter. He turns up LIGHT.)*

MR. HARTMAN. You talked through two double features, Louise.

MRS. HARTMAN. *(Turns off radio, shaking her head)* But I just *can't* understand *why* you would let yourself be trapped into such a foolish arrangement as this. With Clancy's help, that Mrs. Fields *might* win the Flower Show. Then how would you feel?

MR. HARTMAN. *(Patiently)* What's more important—your flowers or your family? I've got Mr. Fields' promise and the contracts are on his desk right now. If he buys a fleet of trucks, we can send Virginia to college in the fall. She can even join a sorority. You don't realize how expensive our offspring are getting. *(They are removing hats, etc.)*

MRS. HARTMAN. Of course I do. *(A trifle petulantly)* But if that Mrs. Fields wins the Flower Show just because Clancy helps her every afternoon—

MR. HARTMAN. If Mrs. Fields wins the Flower Show, I'll never hear the end of it from you. And if Virginia doesn't join a sorority, I'll never hear the end of it from her. (MR. HARTMAN *sits Center chair.*) Raising a family gets to be a darned complex business.

MRS. HARTMAN. *(Moving around room, putting it in order, picking up odd newspapers and magazines)* You'll feel differently on Monday, Jeff. Vacation's half over.

MR. HARTMAN. Where'd Virginia meet this droopy deb— Lord, I'm beginning to talk just like them.

MRS. HARTMAN. *(Smiling)* Shakespeare used the vernacular, Jeff. These kids have added new color to the language.

MR. HARTMAN. You mean you want me to shift gears and get in the groove? Who is this Carollyn, anyway?

(They BOTH laugh.)

MRS. HARTMAN. *(Running her hands through his hair)* Virginia met Carollyn at camp last summer.

MR. HARTMAN. That's what we get for sending our daughter to those fancy summer camps. That girl has descended on this house like a swarm of locusts. What's happening to this family?

MRS. HARTMAN. *(Going to desk and rearranging things)* She's glamour, Jeff. And it's spring, and vacation, and they're all the proper ages.

MR. HARTMAN. Proper ages for *what?*

MRS. HARTMAN. That old man with the long beard is rearing his head again, Jeff. It's love.

MR. HARTMAN. Love, hah! With a juke-box blaring ragtime and the blues and boogie-woogie,—what chance does a delicate emotion like love have?

MRS. HARTMAN. Exactly the same chance it's always had, Jeff.

MR. HARTMAN. *(Rising)* Perhaps. Let's turn in,

shall we? No wonder there are so many broken hearts these days—the old pump is so worn out with the strain of jitterbugging that the first small emotion cracks it wide open. *(PHONE rings. MR. HARTMAN answers it.)* Hello— Yes?— I'll see— *(Calls toward stairs, hand over receiver)* Virginia!

MIDGE. *(Her door flying open, her head sticking out)* Not here. *(Door slams resoundingly.)*

MR. HARTMAN. *(Wincing, back to phone)* She's not here right now. Would you like to leave a message?—Who?—Oh, Christine Myers— *(Repeating message)* It looks as though the club will be able to raise the money for the club pins before Saturday night. Yes— And you'll bring it over to put with the money Virginia has here— Yes, that's clear, Christine, but not so loud, please. The people next door are asleep. (MRS. HARTMAN *laughs.)* —And Joan can't go to the dance with Bill because Bill's going with Maxine—and Maxine broke her date with Philip Finklehoff—but what has all this to do with the club money? (MRS. HARTMAN *is enjoying it.)* Oh, it has *nothing* to do with the money— I'll tell you, Christine—I'll have her call you— No, you better tell her about the track meet yourself— Good night. *(Hangs up; smiles wanly at MRS. HARTMAN.)*

MRS. HARTMAN. *(As they go upstairs)* The dance Saturday night and school again on Monday; things will quiet down, Jeff.

MR. HARTMAN. *(Pausing on stairs)* Dance? Good Lord, I know what that means— Pressing dresses, running errands, telephone calls at the office—

MRS. HARTMAN. *(Laughing, pushing him upstairs)* Jeffrey, you're just not *hep*.

(As soon as they are off, the Left 2 door opens slowly and VIRGINIA *enters, alone and stealthily. From the appearance of her eyes, we can*

guess that she has been crying. She looks around and, reassured that she's alone, crosses to stairway and starts up. MIDGE's *door opens and her head appears.)*

MIDGE. Buzz here?

VIRGINIA. *(Abstractedly)* What?

MIDGE. Buzz, Buzz, Buzz—is he here?

VIRGINIA. *(Near tears)* No, he's *not.* He's at Bradley's. They're all at Bradley's, making fools of themselves.

MIDGE. *(Sympathetic)* You've been crying. Is it Carollyn?

VIRGINIA. *(Nodding)* Carollyn.

MIDGE. Gee, Sis, let's sit down and talk it over. (VIRGINIA *comes downstairs, standing uncertainly at Center chair.* MIDGE, *one hand on back of sofa, leaps sofa, and sits.)* What's the girl equipped with, anyway?

VIRGINIA. I found out a lot of things tonight. I've been blind all week.—She dances with Keith like she knew him all her life, and even Buzz is playing up to her.

MIDGE. Buzz?—I don't believe it.

VIRGINIA. It's true. She went into Bradley's that first night and mowed 'em down.

MIDGE. And Buzz too?—Virginia—

VIRGINIA. Yes? *(Sitting.)*

MIDGE. There's only one thing to do.

VIRGINIA. *(Listlessly)* I think you'd better stay out of it, Midge. I know *your* ideas.

MIDGE. *(Her mind made up)* We've got to get Elliott to take her to the dance.

VIRGINIA. *(Genuinely surprised)* Elliott!

MIDGE. He's the only one left.

VIRGINIA. What about Buzz?

MIDGE. *(Nonchalantly)* Buzz is all tied up.

VIRGINIA. Oh! Odd, he didn't mention—

MIDGE. You go with Keith, and Elliott with Carollyn,—and Buzz with *me*.

VIRGINIA. With you? You're batty.

MIDGE. *(From great heights)* We'll see.

VIRGINIA. You know, when Keith came over the night before last, he came because he was afraid Buzz was going to ask Carollyn—not me.

MIDGE. I know.

VIRGINIA. You *know?*

MIDGE. Sure! I called him on the phone. Because I was afraid you might decide to go with Buzz.

VIRGINIA. *(Rising—crying)* Oh! Oh! *Oh!* I might have known *you* had something to do with it!

(The Left 2 door opens suddenly and CAROLLYN *enters between* KEITH *and* BUZZ. ALL *stop abruptly when they see* VIRGINIA. *General embarrassment. Neither boy moves toward her.)*

CAROLLYN. But she's *here! (Accusingly)* You ran away.

VIRGINIA. I—I had a headache.

MIDGE. Hullo, Buzz! How's the job?

BUZZ. Okay, I guess. Mrs. Fields just assumes I know all about it and lets me go.

VIRGINIA. Oh—I didn't know you were working, Buzz.

BUZZ. No, I didn't think it would be important to you.

CAROLLYN. He told *me* all about it. It sounds but *thrilling*.

VIRGINIA. Oh, he told *you* all about it?

MIDGE. I thought it was to be a secret, Buzz.

(Pause.)

KEITH. *(To make conversation)* Oh, Virginia, I'd like to show you a startling new step I just learned.

VIRGINIA. I've danced all I care to, thank you. *(Suddenly suspicious)* Where'd you learn it?

CAROLLYN. I've been teaching them all, tonight. (VIRGINIA's *anger is rising.*) And I'm not a good dancer a-*tall*, really I'm not.

KEITH. You are too,—distinctly.

CAROLLYN. But I'm not really, really I'm *not* a-tall.

VIRGINIA. *(Bursting out)* Oh, yes, you are. You're *divine! (She storms into sun parlor.)*

(ALL *are puzzled.*)

CAROLLYN. *(Following* VIRGINIA *out—uncertain)* It's terribly sweet of her to say so.

KEITH. *(Following)* I say, Virginia— *(Exits to sun room.)*

MIDGE. *(To* BUZZ—*angry and jealous)* Well, why don't you go with her? That's where you *want* to go.

BUZZ. No, I don't, Midge. *(Looking after the trio in sun room)* I'm just working on a theory. *(Then turns to* MIDGE*)* You know, kid, I want to thank you for fixing me up with that job.

MIDGE. Sometimes I don't know why I did it.

BUZZ. But it looks like I'll have to spend the fifteen bucks on something else. Old man Barry called me today, told me he has a chance to sell that clarinet: the guy's coming back at noon tomorrow, so if I want it I gotta have the fifteen berries by then.

MIDGE. *(Slumps)* Noon!

BUZZ. Not much use of asking Mrs. Fields to pay my salary in advance, so I guess I'll just have to give it up.

MIDGE. *(Excited)* But you can't *do* that, Buzz, not after what I've done,—not after all we've been *through!*

BUZZ. *(Looking at her, smiling)* What can I do?

Dad won't help. And you've done all you can. I give up.

MIDGE. In a pig's eye! I won't *let* you give up. *(Pause. She gets a thought.)* You stay here. I'll get the money. *(Starts for dining room)* Who wants an encyclopedia this day and age? *(Exits.)*

(VIRGINIA *enters from sun parlor, handkerchief to her eyes;* CAROLLYN *follows, handkerchief to her eyes;* KEITH *follows, flapping his arms helplessly.)*

CAROLLYN. *(To* VIRGINIA*)* That's downright insulting. But *absolutely*. It isn't *my* fault a-tall.

KEITH. I'm at a loss.

VIRGINIA. *(To* KEITH, *hotly)* You're always at a loss. You operate on a loss! You're just one big debit sign!

KEITH. *(Weakly)* That's no way to talk.

ELLIOTT. *(Off, in dining room)* No, *no, no!*

(ALL *look toward dining room for a minute.)*

MR. HARTMAN. *(Appears on stairs in robe. With heavy irony and restraint:)* You're home, I hear.

(ALL *are too flabbergasted to reply.)*

ELLIOTT. *(In the dining room)* I said no; I mean no;—and that's final. I wouldn't lend you fifteen dollars if the encyclopedia had never been invented.

(MIDGE *returns—dejected.)*

MR. HARTMAN. My son Elliott, too—his usual self. *(To* VIRGINIA*)* Fifteen dollars—that reminds me. Your so-called friend, the one with the voice of doom—

VIRGINIA. *(Remonstrating)* Father! You mean Christine Myers?

MR. HARTMAN. *(Nods)* She called. Something about the money you're keeping for the Club—for pins.

MIDGE. How much?

VIRGINIA. *(To* MIDGE*)* Never mind.—Thank you, Father.

MR. HARTMAN. M-m-m.—And now I'm going back to bed. I have a busy day tomorrow. I don't expect to sleep, you know— *(With proper sarcasm)* —but I think lying down and listening to your voices is restful. *(Goes off, upstairs.)*

KEITH. Well, good night, Virginia. Uh—good night. *(Goes uneasily out Left 2 door.)*

BUZZ. *(Yawning)* Guess I'll buzz along too. Back hurts a little.

MIDGE. *(Goes to him; takes his hand)* Good night, Buzz.

BUZZ. *(Wincing as she takes his hand)* Ouch!

MIDGE. What?

BUZZ. Blisters. Gardener's blisters.—Good night, kid—and thanks.

MIDGE. Look for me in the morning, Buzz. I'll whistle— *(With a look at* VIRGINIA*)* And I'll *have* it.

BUZZ. Don't rob a bank. *(Turns to* VIRGINIA*)* Anything I can—?

VIRGINIA. Get out. Go away and leave me alone. If I never see you again I'll be as happy as—as—as Solomon!

BUZZ. *(Patting her arm)* Now is that the *technique?*

(VIRGINIA *turns her back to him.* BUZZ *smiles a bit and goes out Left 2.)*

CAROLLYN. That's it—

VIRGINIA. What's what?

CAROLLYN. What you need—*technique*—or a mood—or an approach.

VIRGINIA. I thought—

CAROLLYN. And can I help it because you haven't got it? You treat all boys like your brother.

VIRGINIA. I didn't ask for your advice.

CAROLLYN. I don't mind telling you—I think you're acting horrible and treating me but *terrible!* *(Goes quickly upstairs.)*

VIRGINIA. When she walked into Bradley's, they just swooned. You never saw anything so disgusting in your life.

MIDGE. Virginia—

VIRGINIA. *(She is holding back tears)* Yes?

MIDGE. Can you lend me fifteen dollars for a few days?

VIRGINIA. *(Muffled)* I haven't *got* fifteen dollars.

MIDGE. The club has fifteen dollars.—I heard Dad say—

VIRGINIA. *(Whirling)* You stay away from my dresser. That fifteen-eighty doesn't belong to me. We're saving that for our pins.

MIDGE. When are you going to buy them?

VIRGINIA. We wanted them for the dance on Saturday, but I guess we won't be able to buy them for a couple of weeks.

MIDGE. A couple of weeks?! *(She is moving around the room, her brow furrowed.* VIRGINIA *moves to stairs and starts up.* MIDGE, *crossing to stairs, looks up)* Virginia, do you think there's anything in this *technique* business? Maybe you have to play love like checkers or bridge.

VIRGINIA. You've got to do something— *(Crying, running up the stairs)* —something I haven't been doing.

(MIDGE *returns to Center table, picks up camera,*

puts it around her neck. ELLIOTT *enters from dining room.)*

ELLIOTT. *(Looks around furtively)* I didn't want to come out before. (MIDGE *turns out lamp on table Center—LIGHTS dim.)* Too much noise. Where's Carollyn?

MIDGE. Shh! In her room,—polishing her technique. *(Going to light switch up Left)* Elliott, I don't need your money now. I'm borrowing it elsewhere. But thanks just the same for your belligerent kindness. *(Turns out LIGHTS—dim. Goes up the stairs into her room, slamming door.)*

(ELLIOTT *goes to regard self in mirror. He places pipe in mouth at several angles and he is returning to dining room when* CAROLLYN, *wearing robe, appears on stairs.)*

CAROLLYN. Elliott—

ELLIOTT. *(Turning, surprised)* Carollyn!

CAROLLYN. *(Descending stairs)* I just knew you'd be up, working on your book. I had to talk to *some*body.—You don't know how everyone's been treating me. (ELLIOTT *watches her nervously as she turns out lamp up Right, crosses and sits on sofa.)* Sit here by me, won't you?—Oh, you're smoking your pipe. Men look so handsome with a pipe, but *manly*. (ELLIOTT *sits, pleased.)* Ah, this is so restful. I just seem to run, run, run. And there's really no one I can talk to—*seriously*, I mean. Books, music, *life*—and things.

ELLIOTT. I write better than I talk.—I guess.

CAROLLYN. But I feel so *quiet* with you. *(Leaning her head back.)* There are times when a person wants to get frightfully serious.

ELLIOTT. That's true. I'm that way most of the

time. Of course I think a girl without brains is no person at all.

CAROLLYN. But abso*lute*ly.

ELLIOTT. *(Very serious)* I've known very few girls with any brains.

CAROLLYN. I don't doubt it. I *actually don't doubt it.* So many girls just want to be beautiful.

(WARN Curtain.)

ELLIOTT. *(Taking a breath)* You're beautiful. *(Quoting)* "Is this the face that launched a thousand ships and burned the topless towers of Ilium?"

CAROLLYN. *(Smiling)* Isn't that the *sweetest* thing? Oh, I don't mean I don't think *that's* important too. There's got to be the other side. For instance, golf.

ELLIOTT. What?

CAROLLYN. You write books and play golf *too.* That's the thing I like about you. Let's the two of us, just you and I, play eighteen holes tomorrow.

ELLIOTT. You couldn't make that Saturday, could you?

CAROLLYN. But Saturday's the day of the dance.

ELLIOTT. And about the dance—do you have any plans?

CAROLLYN. It's so *fright*fully confused. Let's don't talk about the dance.

ELLIOTT. What I meant to say was—

CAROLLYN. *(Leaning toward him)* I've needed this talk tonight, Elliott. (MIDGE's *door opens and with camera still around her neck, she stealthily descends stairs and goes behind desk during the following.)* You don't know what a *tonic* you are to one who is just starved for *intellectual* conversation.

ELLIOTT. Carollyn, I never— Well, girls never— I mean to say that *up to now,* women—

CAROLLYN. Do you want to kiss me, Elliott?

ELLIOTT. Well, I—sure I—Carollyn, you don't know what your coming here has meant to me.

(He kisses her once lightly, shyly; sits back, looks at her. Then very definitely kisses her again, as MIDGE raises camera to eye and takes picture. Note: If convenient, MIDGE should use flashlight bulb attachment on camera here. If flashlight is used the following dialogue need not be included, the Curtain falls with ELLIOTT and CAROLLYN turning to MIDGE completely surprised, open-eyed and open-mouthed—for fast Curtain.)

CAROLLYN. What was that?

(MIDGE has ducked behind the desk, out of sight.)

ELLIOTT. Don't spoil it.

(PHONE rings. Before either can reach it, MIDGE pops up from behind desk, takes phone, and very brightly:)

MIDGE. This is Midge.

THE CURTAIN HAS FALLEN

ACT TWO

SCENE III

SCENE: *The same.*

TIME: *Late Friday afternoon.*

AT RISE: *In various positions on the floor are water glasses, lying flat.* ELLIOTT, *wearing* MR. HARTMAN'S *old golf knickers of a bright plaid design—very baggy on* ELLIOTT—*stands below Center table swinging a golf club (putter) at an imagin-*

ary golf ball. He swings a few. His pipe is in his mouth and he wears his glasses. He is not conscious of the ludicrous picture he presents. He swings the club a couple of times, then reaches into his pockets—very deep—and pulls out two golf balls; drops them to floor. He assumes a putting position and attempts to putt one ball into the glass lying at down Left leg of sofa—ball going at an angle upstage. Needless to say, he misses. He goes over and precisely rearranges glasses, returns to former position and tries again. VIRGINIA, *a towel wrapped around her head and an eyelash curler held in her left hand and curling the lashes on her left eye, enters from dining room, gives* ELLIOTT *one doleful look and goes up to foot of stairs.*

ELLIOTT. *(Golf club nonchalantly over shoulder)* Where is she, Virginia?

VIRGINIA. Tennis. *(Wails)* With Keith. *(Stamps upstairs and off.)*

ELLIOTT. *(Looking after her)* Oh. *(He returns to his game.)*

EDNA. *(Enters from dining room singing)*
  "And every breath becomes a sigh,
  Not a sigh of despair, but a sign that I—
    (Looks up, then flatly:)
  care."
I better get those glasses back before dinner. *(Takes a step toward him just as he swings club. She steps back.)* Right in the sand trap. It don't mean a thing if you ain't got that swing.

CLANCY. *(Enters from sun parlor)* Psst! Edna—

EDNA. *(Going to him)* Clancy, I thought you were at Mrs. Fields'. Did she fire you?

CLANCY. *(Unthinking)* I been fishing.

EDNA. Fishing!?

CLANCY. *(Confused)* I mean—digging for fishing

worms. Mr. Fields likes to fish. *(He pleases himself with the lie.)* —Where's Midge?

EDNA. Don't ask me where any member of *this* family is.

CLANCY. You know the way to solve all this is for you to marry me.

EDNA. That's not a very romantic proposal.— Right here in broad daylight! *(Whisping on to sun parlor)* And what about my career?

CLANCY. *(Helplessly to* ELLIOTT*)* You got your Dad's pants on? (ELLIOTT *looks up with a glare— doesn't answer.* CLANCY, *making conversation:)* Golf's a good game, I guess— *(As he goes into sun parlor)* —Seems kinda pointless, though, chasin' a little ball for miles and miles.

(ELLIOTT *looks up and is thinking this over when the Left 2 door opens and* CAROLLYN, *dressed for tennis, her hair caught up in a snood, enters. She pauses as she sees* ELLIOTT; *smothers a giggle.* ELLIOTT *looks up; quickly removes glasses. Places them on Center table.)*

ELLIOTT. *(With his old stiffness)* I understood you were playing tennis—with Keith Nolan.

CAROLLYN. *(Coming down in back of sofa)* He won three sets. He's not a gentleman.

ELLIOTT. *(Definitely tackling the problem)* Carollyn, we must come to some kind of an understanding. You can't play tennis with Keith on Friday and golf with me on Saturday.

CAROLLYN. Oh, Elliott, you're jealous.

ELLIOTT. Jealousy is beneath me. But I'd much prefer your playing with girls. You know, Carollyn, after last night, after the way you kissed me—well —I may be presumptuous—

CAROLLYN. You're sweet.

MIDGE. *(The Left 2 door bursts open and* MIDGE, *waving a set of photographs in her hand, comes breezily into the room. To* ELLIOTT *directly)* Hot foot it out of here, Romeo. I've got business with this cool drip of water.

ELLIOTT. What did you say?

MIDGE. *(Translating)* Go upstairs, go downstairs, go in my lady's chamber—And for gosh sakes, take off Dad's pants.

ELLIOTT. *(Thoroughly embarrassed)* All right, I'll go. *(To* MIDGE*)* I've analyzed you thoroughly, young lady. You're just a mass of irreconcilable complexes and if you don't amalgamate them, you're going to explode. *(Goes upstairs.)*

CAROLLYN. I'd better go change.

MIDGE. Grab hold of thin air, Duchess, and prepare yourself for a cataclysm.

CAROLLYN. Well, really—

MIDGE. Miss Webster, you came here flying a false flag. You've given my sister an emotional hemorrhage. You've made Keith go under for the third time, hook-line-and-sinker; and you've even got Buzz slap-happy. Now—who's taking you to the Prom?

CAROLLYN. But, Midgie—

MIDGE. This is no time to Midgie me.

CAROLLYN. But my dear, I *don't* know what you're talking about.

MIDGE. I'm talking about you having all *three* poor masculine fish flopping on your line.

CAROLLYN. *(Rising)* Everyone's hurling all the blame on me. But absolutely! Can I help it if I have appeal?

MIDGE. *(Thinking)* Appeal?—Is *that* what you call it?

CAROLLYN. But of course that's it. I've spent years developing it and I should know.

MIDGE. Want to see some pictures?

CAROLLYN. *(Looking suspiciously at pictures)* Why, those are mine! You took my camera—

MIDGE. Had the whole roll developed. Do you realize that in thirty-six pictures there are fourteen dopes swooning over that moon face of yours? You're an unmarried bigamist.

CAROLLYN. *(Evenly)* What are you going to do with those photos? They belong to *me*.

MIDGE. Unless you play the game according to Hoyle—need I say more?

CAROLLYN. You mean you'll show them to Keith?

MIDGE. *(Understanding)* Keith?—So it's really *Keith!* Say, Keith is personal property—Virginia's. He's her territory and I won't see him invaded.

CAROLLYN. I'll buy those pictures from you, dear.

MIDGE. I don't need money *now*. Well, do you go with Elliott?

CAROLLYN. *(Dubiously)* Can he dance?

MIDGE. You've been teaching everybody else, teach him.

CAROLLYN. You know, Midge, this is no way to make friends.

MIDGE. I'm just developing a "technique," Duchess.

CAROLLYN. *(Going upstairs)* I'll think it over.

MIDGE. Tonight's the deadline. (CAROLLYN *is gone.* MIDGE, *whistling, goes into dining room and as she returns, biting into an apple,* MRS. HARTMAN *enters Left 2.)* Mother, has Gabby called?

MRS. HARTMAN. Not while I've been here, dear.

MIDGE. Not all day? *(She bites into apple.)*

MRS. HARTMAN. Gabby isn't sick, is she, dear?

MIDGE. *(Waving hand)* Men.

MRS. HARTMAN. The same old story.

MIDGE. Mmmmm.—Mother, would you say I had what it takes? *(Bites into apple.)*

MRS. HARTMAN. *(Puzzled)* What it takes, Midge?

MIDGE. *(Her brow furrowed)* The way I look at it, a girl's simply got to find out.

Mrs. Hartman. Has your father come home yet?
—A girl's got to find out what?

Midge. *(Slowly)* Whether she has it or whether she hasn't.

Mrs. Hartman. *(Patiently)* Has what, dear?

Midge. *(Looking up sharply)* Oh, Mother, don't be obtuse, please.

Mrs. Hartman. *(At a loss)* I'll try my best.

Midge. *(Explaining)* —Whatever it takes to make a boy do handsprings and cartwheels and nip-ups and all the crazy things they *do* do if you've got it!

Mrs. Hartman. *(Concealing her smile)* Oh—I'm beginning to understand in a vague way.

Midge. Well, I think if a girl hasn't got it, she's got to know how to get it.

Mrs. Hartman. I see.

Midge. And if she *has* got it—well—she's got to know what to *do* with it, doesn't she?

Mrs. Hartman. I think you're a very nice young lady just as you are, Midge.

Midge. Nice!? You have to be more than a *nice young lady,* let me tell you!

(KNOCK at Left 2 door.)

Mrs. Hartman. *(Crosses to dining room)* Come help me with the salad, Midge, and we'll decide what you can do with it. *(Exits.)*

(Midge opens Left 2 door and Keith steps warily over the threshold.)

Midge. Hi, Keith! *(Goes to stairway)* Virginia come down. And if you've got anything on your face, take it off.

Keith. But you see, I came to see—

Midge. She'll be with you in a sec. Park the dignified carcass. *(Goes to dining room and out.)*

(KEITH *does not sit down and* VIRGINIA *descends stairs.*)

VIRGINIA. Oh!

KEITH. How do you do, Virginia?

VIRGINIA. Are you sure you wanted to see *me?*

KEITH. Can't we be amicable?

VIRGINIA. I'm sure I don't know what you mean, Mr. Nolan.

KEITH. Don't you?

VIRGINIA. I'm sure there are other people who are *much* more attractive— Playing tennis—*all* afternoon—in the *sun*—drinking cokes— *(She is working herself up)* —laughing—the whole *live-long afternoon! (Whirls on him)* —And if you want to break our date for tomorrow night, *now's* the time to do it, Mr. Nolan.

KEITH. You're a fiery creature.

VIRGINIA. Don't be cryptic. Certain people from New York might like cryptic people, but I don't.

KEITH. I was only trying to entertain *your* guest.

VIRGINIA. You've entertained her! You've entertained her all over town, and the whole Senior Class is practically laughing in my face. I can see it all.

KEITH. *(Turning away)* Here we go again. *(Sits on sofa.)*

VIRGINIA. And you can sit down! *(He stands up quickly)* You're the cause of it. If you didn't have the kind of heart that turned color every time you saw a pretty face—and I don't think her face *is* pretty—well, I'm coming to the conclusion that you're not the man for me, Keith Nolan, and I don't know *how* I'll ever be able to face anybody! *(Runs off upstairs, meets* CAROLLYN *who is coming down, glares at her and dashes off)* Ohhh!!

CAROLLYN. *(Looking after her)* I honestly can't understand what's gotten into everybody in this house.

KEITH. This is deucedly embarrassing.
CAROLLYN. *(Coming to him)* Why, "Curly"?
KEITH. *(His hand unconsciously climbs to his head)* I haven't asked her—but she thinks I'm taking her to the Prom.
CAROLLYN. *(Remembering* MIDGE*)* Well, aren't you?
KEITH. What!?
CAROLLYN. You know I haven't really given my answer yet, to anyone.
KEITH. But you as much as said—you as much as told me—
CAROLLYN. But, Curly, *(Endearingly)* something has come up. *(Another thought strikes her. She becomes enticing and quiet)* Keith, you've been around enough to realize that a girl—in my position—has to do certain things—that is, go places and do things she really doesn't want to do.
KEITH. *(Playing the sophisticate)* I realize that.
CAROLLYN. And that these other things would *naturally* involve young men—going places with young men.
KEITH. *(A little uncertainly now)* Before you met me, you mean?
CAROLLYN. Oh, yes. And if you should suddenly learn that I had gone out with boys whom I simply *loathed*, you'd understand, wouldn't you?
KEITH. *(Magnanimously)* I think so. In fact, I'm *sure* of it.
CAROLLYN. Then if someone should show you some pictures, pictures that I wasn't sure you should see—before I knew your attitude, of course—you wouldn't *dislike* me, would you— *(Coyly)* Curly?
KEITH. *(His hand again slipping up to his hair)* I *couldn't* dislike *you*, Carollyn.
CAROLLYN. Then I guess I really won't have to go with Elliott after all.

KEITH. Do you mean to tell me that Elliott tried to force you to go to the dance with him?
ELLIOTT. *(Dressed as before, comes down the stairs. He has his glasses on)* Was that my name you were bandying about, Mr. Nolan?
KEITH. Yes, it was. Do you mean to tell me you had the insufferable nerve to try to force your will on this young lady?
ELLIOTT. Listen, actor, have you ever read a play written later than 1900?
CAROLLYN. Keith, you really don't understand.
KEITH. I understand well enough. This greasy grind gets romantic ideas and now he wants to step all over your feet;—and nothing is too low, not even filthy blackmail,—
CAROLLYN. Curly, let me explain—
ELLIOTT. *(Removing glasses)* What did you say? —Everyone has always called me a *greasy grind*. Although I do not believe in corporal punishment as a rule, when you encounter a brain which would not comprehend a subtle insult, it is the only way. *(Is rolling up his sleeves.)*
CAROLLYN. What are you going to do?
ELLIOTT. I am going to teach this empty-headed imbecile that a greasy grind can also lose his temper. *(Now assumes the exaggerated pose from earlier scene.)*
KEITH. Come out in the back yard.
ELLIOTT. And let's not get vulgar about it.
CAROLLYN. You can't do this. If you'd but let me explain.

(KEITH *gives* ELLIOTT *a shove.* ELLIOTT *turns on him in pose.)*

ELLIOTT. Don't shove me— *(Mockingly)* "Curly."
KEITH. Wait till we get outside—I'll *really* shove you. *(They exit through sun parlor.)*

CAROLLYN. *(Following)* I really didn't think you two were the cave men type.

(As soon as they are off stage, a CLARINET can be heard playing off Left.)

MIDGE. *(Dashes in from dining room, crosses to Left 2 door. Suddenly she remembers herself, places the apple she carries on top of the radio, reaches for her hair, pulls it down the side of her face—*CAROLLYN*-fashion—crosses down to sofa, picks up magazine and when* BUZZ *knocks, calls:)* Come in.

BUZZ. *(Enters. If possible, he can still be playing clarinet)* Hullo, kid!

MIDGE. *(Rising)* But, Buzz, how nice!

BUZZ. Got it. I'm gonna miss Hotspur for a while, but isn't she a beauty? *(Holds up clarinet.)*

MIDGE. Very nice, I'm sure.

BUZZ. *(Looking up at her, sees her hair)* Just washed your hair?

MIDGE. *(Smiling crookedly)* Oh, no, I'm going to wear it like this from now on. More sophisticated, don't you think?

BUZZ. I guess so.

MIDGE. Sit down here, Buzz. *(Indicates place on sofa, next to her.* BUZZ *sits, playing a few notes on clarinet.)* I think music is rather uplifting, don't you?

BUZZ. *(The music stops abruptly)* Come again—?

MIDGE. Buzz, now you have it, don't you—the clarinet? Just like I said.

BUZZ. Y-yes.

MIDGE. And Buzz—

BUZZ. Um-hum?

MIDGE. Well, do you still *feel* the same?

BUZZ. I'm tired. Gardening's tough work.—Oh, I'll pay you the fifteen on Tuesday, Midge.

Midge. Perish the thought! Any time will do—within two weeks.

Buzz. Mrs. Fields will pay me Tuesday. But why two weeks?

Midge. —Because in two weeks the sub-debs— *(Dismissing it)* Buzz, as I was walking over to your house this morning, I kept thinking—

Buzz. Now Midge, do we have to—?

Midge. Oh, no—that's all over. I must have been dreadfully adolescent, all that gibberish about my evening gown—it's white, Buzz—sort of whitish blue—anyway, I must have been disgusting. But that was years ago, the way I reckon time.

Buzz. *(Teasing)* Time flies, doesn't it?

Midge. Buzz, you haven't asked Carollyn to the Prom, have you?

Buzz. I'm not quite sure, Midge. I'm not quite sure about anything. *(Laughs)* Old Chinese proverb.

(KNOCK at Left 2 door.)

Midge. It's pale blue, Buzz. Shall I show you? I'll run up and try it on.

Buzz. Say, Midge, you don't mean—?

Midge. *(Desperately)* Buzz— *(Almost a caress)* Buzz— *(Her eyes are fastened on his, her emotions evident.)*

(KNOCK repeated.)

Buzz. Hadn't you better—?
Midge. I'd better.

(They do not move. Buzz embarrassed.)

Buzz. Then maybe I'd—

(KNOCK—loud.)

MIDGE. Darn! Darnation! *(Goes to Left 2 door, the spell broken)* Great leaping morons!

(She angrily flings door open, displaying CHRISTINE MYERS. *She wears, if convenient, her gym bloomers with a boy's dirty sweat shirt above. May wear regular skirt and sweat shirt. A moment's pause.)*

CHRISTINE. *(Low, intense)* What did you call me?

MIDGE. Nothing to what I could call you!

CHRISTINE. Tell Virginia I want her. And snap it up—I been shot-putting and I've got to get home for a shower.

MIDGE. *(At bottom of stairs)* Virginia!—Christine here, and foaming at the mouth.

VIRGINIA. *(Off)* Be right down.

MIDGE. *(To* BUZZ *with a glance at* CHRISTINE*)* As I was saying, how do you get along with Mrs. Fields?

BUZZ. It's hard to say. She just looks at me and tells me I probably know what to do and sometimes she shakes her head and says, "And Mrs. Hartman wins the flower shows."—Some kind of a joke, I guess.

VIRGINIA. *(Descends stairs. In her hand she carries ice cubes wrapped in a towel; these she applies to her reddened eyes during subsequent action.)* Hello, Christine!

CHRISTINE. *(More than a little angry at* MIDGE*)* I came for the money, Virginia.

VIRGINIA. So soon?

CHRISTINE. Didn't your father tell you?

MIDGE. *(Alarmed)* The club money?

VIRGINIA. He didn't say a word. Come on upstairs and you can explain. We'll get the money too. It's up here.—Oh, how do you do, Mr. Lindsay?

BUZZ. Hello! You always looked best just after a good cry.

VIRGINIA. Coming, Christine?
CHRISTINE. Coming.—I told your father on the phone last night—

(CHRISTINE *follows* VIRGINIA *upstairs—clumping rather loudly.*)

MIDGE. Gosh, gosh, oh golly gosh, Buzz!
MR. HARTMAN. (*Enters Left 2, carrying the evening paper. Surveying room, speaks gratefully*) My, things are quiet. Hello, Buzz.

(*Goes to* MIDGE, *hugs her to him. She draws away. He looks at her, surprised.*)

MIDGE. (*Very worried*) Don't, Father.
MR. HARTMAN. What's this? Why all the frowns? Deep furrows from little furrows, you know.
MIDGE. I know.—Dad, can I count on you to stick by me? Can I?

(MR. HARTMAN *and* BUZZ *exchange a look.*)

MR. HARTMAN. Well, well, well, I can't get over how quiet it is here today. Wish it could always be like this.

(*There are CALLS off stage Right, far away.*)

BOYS' VOICES. (*Off*)
Fight!
Hey, Red, come see the fight!
Get your tickets right here, right here.
Funniest thing you ever saw!
GIRLS' VOICES. (*Off*)
Make them stop.
Ohhhhhhh!
Hit him!
Hit him again!

(These voices are mingled together and only a few of the sentences are heard distinctly. BUZZ goes to sun parlor door. MR. HARTMAN follows; looks over shoulder.)

MR. HARTMAN. I knew it couldn't last— Probably a couple of ruffians in the alley.

(MIDGE makes a dash for the Left 2 door, then she remembers herself, straightens, and comes back into room. VIRGINIA dashes down stairs, not in tears but her voice shrill and worried. CHRISTINE follows, puzzled.)

VIRGINIA. I've been robbed!

(MIDGE, who has just started to sit down on chair, down Left, leaps to her feet before she reaches the chair.)

MR. HARTMAN. What do you mean?
VIRGINIA. Somebody's taken all but eighty cents of my club money!
MR. HARTMAN. *(Disbelieving)* Why would they leave eighty cents? You must have put it some place else.
VIRGINIA. *(Desperately)* I *didn't!* I had it in my dresser drawer; and, Daddy, it's not my money!
MR. HARTMAN. Quiet now, quiet. I don't think anyone could get in the house.
CHRISTINE. *(Threatening)* I'd like to have whoever did it here right now. *(Wrings an imaginary neck.)*
VIRGINIA. We wanted to buy the pins before the dance.
CHRISTINE. Fifteen dollars! That's grand larceny.
MIDGE. I thought you said two weeks.

ACT II AND CAME THE SPRING

(ALL *turn to her.*)

VIRGINIA. *(Wailing accusingly)* She took it!

MR. HARTMAN. Now don't start accusing your sister.

VIRGINIA. She took it. I can tell by her face.

BUZZ. *(To* MIDGE*)* So that's where you got that fifteen dollars?

VIRGINIA. What have you got to do with this?

BUZZ. She loaned me the fifteen.

MR. HARTMAN. *(At a loss)* I'd better get your mother.

VIRGINIA. *(To* BUZZ*)* I can't believe it. It's bad enough—my own sister a thief, but you her accomplice!

MIDGE. I was gonna pay it back. It was just a loan.

VIRGINIA. My own sister!

MR. HARTMAN. Virginia, stop that. *(Calls in dining room door)* Louise, for Pete's sake, come in here.

MIDGE. *(Desperately to* BUZZ*)* But you got your gobstick.

BUZZ. *(A trifle angry)* Why the heck didn't you tell me?

(KNOCK at the Left 2 door.)

MR. HARTMAN. Now what? *(Goes to door, opens it.* MR. *and* MRS. FIELDS *are there.)* Why, come in, Mr. Fields.

(MR. *and* MRS. FIELDS *enter.* MRS. FIELDS *is a buxom woman in her 40's with a will of iron and determination written across her face.* MR. FIELDS *is a gentle, be-mustached man, a little older than* MRS. FIELDS, *small in stature, an excellent business man, but inclined to obsequiousness in the presence of his wife.)*

Mrs. Fields. *(Pointing to* Buzz*)* There he is! *(To* Mr. Hartman*)* Do you call that boy a *gardener?*

Mr. Fields. I'm sorry, Mr. Hartman,— This is my wife, Mrs. Fields—Mr. Hartman.

Mrs. Fields. This is no time for amenities. Mr. Hartman, *did* you or did you *not* send this young man over to my house to *deliberately* tear up my garden?

Mr. Hartman. Buzz?

Alan. *(Enters the Left 2 door, which has been left open)* Hello,. Midge!

Mrs. Fields. Alan, I told you not to come.

Alan. But Mother, this is so silly.

Mr. Feilds. I quite agree.

Mrs. Fields. *(To* Mr. Hartman*)* Will you answer my question?

Buzz. I think I can explain.

Mrs. Hartman. *(Enters from dining room; sees crowd. Speaks cheerfully.)* Well, well, well!

Mr. Fields. Good evening, Mrs. Hartman.

Mrs. Fields. *(Witheringly)* It's hard to believe, Mrs. Hartman, it's hard to believe that you would stoop to such a *low* trick to win a flower show.

Mrs. Hartman. *(Freezing)* I'm afraid I don't understand, Mrs. Fields.

Mrs. Fields. Don't act innocent.

Alan. Mother, why not let Dad handle this?

Mrs. Fields. Your father never handled anything in his life. (Midge *has sunk miserably into the chair down Left.* Virginia, *concerned with her own affairs, is near tears and glaring at* Midge.*)* You sent this young man over to my house to wreck my garden, and *believe you me,* he succeeded.

Buzz. What did I do?

Mrs. Hartman. Mrs. Fields, *Buzz* isn't our gardener.

Mrs. Fields. You're not telling me *that!* Do you

know what he did? He viciously yanked out my most expensive and beautiful bulbs!
Buzz. Bulbs? Those?

(The sounds of the FIGHT grow louder off.)

Alan. What's that?

(All *turn to him as though he has spoken in church.*)

Mrs. Hartman. But *Clancy* is our gardener. I distinctly told him myself— *(Goes to* Buzz*)* Buzz, have you been tending Mrs. Fields' flowers?
Midge. *(Miserably)* I thought it was an easy job.

(Mr. *and* Mrs. Hartman *look at each other for a blank moment, then* Both *comprehend.* All *turn to* Midge.)

Mr. Hartman. Midge!
Mrs. Hartman. Midge!   *(Together)*
Virginia. Midge!
Midge. *(Unutterably miserable, but with hope, to* Mrs. Fields*)* But you're going to pay him, aren't you?
Mrs. Fields. Pay him!!!! *(She nearly explodes.)*
Mr. Fields. Now, Cecelia—
Mrs. Fields. *He's* going to pay *me!*

(Buzz *glares at* Midge.)

Mr. Hartman. How much is it, Mrs. Fields? You'll get my check in the morning.
Mrs. Fields. It's not the money—
Buzz. *(To* Mr. Hartman*)* I'll pay you back, Mr. Hartman, honest. I don't know how, but I will. *(Looks sadly down at his clarinet.)*

Mrs. Fields. Not really the money—it's the *principle* of the thing. It's the most unethical affair I have ever heard of.

Mrs. Hartman. *(A bit angrily)* There is nothing unethical about it. *(Gives* Midge *a look)* It's merely a childish mistake, made by a child, and if you can't see it as such, I'm sorry. How much do we owe you?

Mrs. Fields. The actual damage is only about six dollars—but it's the *principle*.

Mr. Hartman. *(Sarcastically)* Well, how much is the principle worth?

Mrs. Fields. *(Turning to* Mr. Fields*)* How you could even *think* of doing business with people like this— "How much is a principle worth!!?"

Mr. Fields. *(To* Mr. Hartman*)* I'm afraid, Mr. Hartman, that under the circumstances— *(Darts glance to his wife)* —I suppose it will be impossible for us to go through with our little deal.

Mr. Hartman. *Little* deal! Mr. Fields, don't tell me you'd—cancel your order for the trucks—!!

Alan. Whatever it is, he'll do what she says. He always does.

(At this point Clancy *and* Edna *enter from sun parlor with a disheveled and much-battered* Elliott *between them. His clothes are torn, he is bruised, one eye is black, but his spirit is unbroken.)*

Elliott. I could have kept going all night.
Mrs. Hartman. Elliott!
Mr. Hartman. Son!
Midge. Oh!— *(Together)*
Mrs. Fields. Your son!?
Buzz. For cat's sake!

Clancy. They've been at it for nearly half an hour. He's not hurt, but he's sure worn out.

(ELLIOTT *collapses to sofa again, utterly exhausted.* VIRGINIA *tears upstairs.* MR. HARTMAN *shakes head.* MRS. HARTMAN *rushes back to* ELLIOTT. CHRISTINE *is making for the Left 2 door—heavily—as*

THE CURTAIN FALLS

ACT II AND CAME THE SPRING 107

(They help ELLIOTT *to sofa and regard him.* MRS. HARTMAN *takes his head solicitously.)*

(WARN Curtain.)

MRS. FIELDS. Who are these people?

BUZZ. He's the real gardener.

CLANCY. Is this that Mrs. Fields?

MRS. FIELDS. Indeed I am! And believe me I've seen quite enough! *(To* MR. FIELDS*)* Coming, Link?

MR. FIELDS. Yes, dear. Mr. Hartman, I'll—I'll send the contracts back in the morning.

(As they are about to leave, GABBY *enters Left 2 door, which is still ajar, wades through the crowd, goes directly to* MIDGE.*)*

GABBY. I just came over to tell you, Midge Hartman—I went into Bradley's and Freddie cut me dead—he just picked up his Seven Up and walked away. *(She is near tears and she runs out Left 2)* And it's all your fault!

MRS. FIELDS. Come, Link. Come, Alan. A disgusting exhibition! *(She goes Left 2.)*

(MR. FIELDS *gives an embarrassed look to* MR. HARTMAN *and follows.)*

ALAN. Sorry, Midge. That's the way she is. Sorry, Buzz. *(Exits Left 2.)*

CHRISTINE. *(From landing)* This is better than a football game.

ELLIOTT. *(Rising, looking at* MIDGE*)* Is it true, Midge? *Did* you try to blackmail Carollyn into going with *me?*

VIRGINIA. I'll never be able to hold my head up again as long as I live.

MIDGE. I was only trying to help. *(Breaks down.)* I was only trying to help everybody. Gosh, I'll be glad when I'm not *young* any more.

ACT THREE

Scene: *Same.*

Time: *Saturday evening, a little after eight o'clock.*

At Rise: Mrs. Hartman *is sitting at desk and* Mr. Hartman *stands at open Left 2 door, leaning, looking out in an abstracted manner. Both expressions show very plainly the effects of their week.*

Mr. Hartman. I can't help remembering—you said, if we ever get into any *real* trouble, count on the kids.

Mrs. Hartman. *(Wearily)* That's what I said.

Mr. Hartman. Count on them to get us into it.— Which one of us will have the privilege of telling Virginia she can't go to college?

Mrs. Hartman. Is that what it really means, Jeff? Is it that serious?

Mr. Hartman. There's no other outfit in town that needs a whole fleet of trucks and unless we can get Midge to blow up all the trucks in town, I really don't think we have a chance.

Mrs. Hartman. *(Smiling in spite of herself)* That's terrible.

Mr. Hartman. Where's son Elliott?

Mrs. Hartman. In his room. He doesn't feel very well.

Mr. Hartman. He'll probably ache for days. I know what that first scrap means.

Mrs. Hartman. *(Alarmed at the idea)* First!—Well, Jeff, he seems to have struck that happy balance you were talking about—but he's not so happy about it.

Mr. Hartman. *(Really concerned, comes behind sofa)* Good Lord, you don't suppose *I* had anything to do with that?

Mrs. Hartman. You said you'd give five hundred dollars to see him dash out of here with a ball bat over his shoulder.

Mr. Hartman. *(Smiling crookedly)* Maybe he should have gone out there yesterday with a ball bat over his shoulder.

Edna. *(Enters from dining room. She no longer wears her uniform; she wears a frilly white dress. She speaks haughtily)* Have those two debutantes thought up anything else for me to press?

Mrs. Hartman. I'm sorry they've been such a bother, Edna. You know what it's like on dance nights.

Edna. I probably know better than *anybody* in this house. Midge's dress is ready too—just in case.

Mrs. Hartman. Just in case what? Midge isn't going to the dance.

Edna. I've heard those final statements before.

(Mr. Hartman *grins.*)

Mrs. Hartman. Thanks very much, Edna. This is one time we won't be wheedled.

Edna. *(Cynically)* Yes, Mrs. Hartman. *(Returns to dining room.)*

Mr. Hartman. What's got into *her?*

Mrs. Hartman. She's been working pretty hard.

Mr. Hartman. What's she all dressed up for?

Mrs. Hartman. *(Continuing)* And I suspect she's angry because I had to let Clancy go.

Mr. Hartman. Adolescence may have been the

same in caves, but you've got to admit family life's a good deal more complicated these days.

(MIDGE *enters Left 2 door. She leans for a moment against the frame. She wears her sweater and skirt.* MR. *and* MRS. HARTMAN *say nothing.* MR. HARTMAN *sits in chair Center.* MIDGE *looks at them a moment, then comes down between them.*)

MIDGE. I paid Mrs. Fields her money. *(Pause)* Sold my camera. *(Pause)* That woman is almost as adamant as *you* are. (MR. *and* MRS. HARTMAN *exchange glances.*) Mrs. Fields kept saying it wasn't the money, it was the principle of the thing—but she kept the money.
MRS. HARTMAN. Then there's nothing more to be said. *(Crosses to desk; sits.)*
MIDGE. You'd think I had leprosy— Mother— (MR. HARTMAN *reads his paper.*) What will Clancy do without a job?
MRS. HARTMAN. Clancy is old enough to learn that everything he does has its consequences.
MIDGE. *(Eagerly over to desk)* But it wasn't his fault.
MRS. HARTMAN. Even Clancy should learn what responsibility means. *(Adds)* It doesn't matter now, anyway. I won't need a gardener after I drop out of the Garden Club.
MIDGE. *(Hurt)* Mother!
MRS. HARTMAN. After all, Mrs. Fields will tell everyone in town that I plotted to uproot her precious garden. Virginia isn't the only one who'll have to face disgrace.
MIDGE. *(Contrite and touching the depths of unhappiness)* Mother, didn't Dad write a check for her?

Mrs. Hartman. He did, but that doesn't in any way relieve either of you of the responsibility.

Mr. Hartman. *(Reading paper)* Louise, I think this responsibility business is highly overrated. *(Taps paper)* Look at Congress.

(Midge *flashes him a grateful look.*)

Mrs. Hartman. Jeff, you raise old Ned about everything the children do, but if I'd let you, you'd turn around and let them have their own way every time.

Mr. Hartman. *(Rising, taking paper, goes to stairs)* I can't help remembering how important a dance was to us at that age.

Mrs. Hartman. *(Goes to* Midge, *puts her arm around her, hugs her briefly)* I remember too, Jeff. That's what makes it just as hard on me as it is on them.

Midge. *(After a moment)* Mother, you know what we were talking about—?

Mrs. Hartman. It seems we've talked about a great deal the last several days.

Midge. That about what it takes to make a boy do cartwheels. (Mrs. Hartman *looks up, puzzled.*) Well, it doesn't matter, about the dance anyway, because *I just don't have it.* *(Throws herself on sofa dejectedly.)*

Mr. Hartman. *(From stairs)* Come along, Louise—before the dance bombs start exploding in your face.

(Mrs. Hartman, *with a sympathetic look at* Midge, *follows* Mr. Hartman *upstairs.*)

Midge. *(Crosses to phone, picks it up, whispers her number as she nervously glances at the various entrances. Into phone)* Humbolt 224— May I speak with Mrs. Fields, please?—This is Midge Hartman— *(Her face brightening a bit)* —Yes, Alan— Oh, she won't talk to me?—I want to tell you, Alan, it's very kind of you to take so much interest. Thanks for trying to explain— (ELLIOTT *comes down the stairs. He has an ice bag on his head, held with one hand, and his other hand is moving over his sore jaw with tenderness. His black eye is now a light gray, but his face and demeanor betray his physical weariness and his mental confusion.* MIDGE, *into phone)* Thank you, Alan, very much. I'd like to see you *too* sometime. Bye-bye. (MIDGE *looks up, catches sight of* ELLIOTT) Hurt, Elliott? (ELLIOTT *flashes her a look)* Your eye's not so black now. (ELLIOTT *is crossing toward dining room.)* The beefsteak did it, huh? *(Suddenly)* Elliott, I think it was good for you, and I'm sorry if you don't think so too.

ELLIOTT. *(Looks up sharply as he reaches dining room door)* I'm in no position to think so.

MIDGE. *(With some of her old enthusiasm)* But don't you see, you're not a bookworm any more. Now you can write, be happy, and have dates like other boys.

ELLIOTT. I'm glad you think I can be happy. However, you have presented me with a thought, and I shall consider it.

(As he continues in dining room, PHONE rings.
MIDGE crosses to it, with something less than her usual agility.)

MIDGE. This is Midge. *(But somehow her voice doesn't sound the same. She stiffens suddenly)* Yes, Buzz? *(She slumps)* —Oh, I'll call her, if you're sure— *(Listens hopefully, but evidently* BUZZ *is sure. She lays phone down gingerly and goes to stairs)* Virginia!! Telephone!

VIRGINIA. *(Off)* I'll take it up here. Please hang up down there.

(MIDGE *returns to phone but she cannot resist listening. She listens for several moments, her face showing the following emotions in turn: surprise, anger, then utter hopelessness and dejection. She replaces receiver. Tears in her eyes.* MRS. HARTMAN *comes downstairs and finds* MIDGE *sitting on desk, weeping bitterly. She goes to her, places her hand on shoulder.)*

MIDGE. *(Muffled)* She's making him take Carrollyn. And Buzz told her everything was just the same between them. *(Looks up)* Mother, Buzz really cares for Virginia.

MRS. HARTMAN. Why, yes, dear. That's one of the things you had to learn for yourself.

MIDGE. *(Miserably)* I wish I'd never known it.

MRS. HARTMAN. You should be glad.

MIDGE. Glad? How can I—?

MRS. HARTMAN. Because you're just about ready to grow up now, Midge—

MIDGE. I don't know whether I want to or not, if this is what it means.

MRS. HARTMAN. This is what it means. Harsh facts, sometimes, and bitter facts, and disappointments.

MIDGE. Disappointment? That's all you think it is!

MRS. HARTMAN. It's more than that for me, Midge. *(Furtively watches for a reaction.)*

MIDGE. *(Lifting her head)* You?

MRS. HARTMAN. Oh, I don't mean the Garden Club, or Virginia's college, or your father's business—

MIDGE. No—?

MRS. HARTMAN. No—I mean you, Midge. The kid herself.

MIDGE. You mean I'm a disappointment—to you? Is that it?

MRS. HARTMAN. That's it.

MIDGE. *(Shows her unhappiness. Her lip trembles)* I'm sorry, Mother.

MRS. HARTMAN. Disappointed, Midge—*not* in what you've done, which was foolish—but in what prompted it—

MIDGE. It was just—Buzz—I—I loved him, I think.

MRS. HARTMAN. No, I think it was selfishness—

MIDGE. Oh, no—

MRS. HARTMAN. Selfishness that prompted the whole thing. The blind selfishness of a little girl who's not trying very hard to be a—woman.

MIDGE. But I am. Don't you see—I *am* trying.

MRS. HARTMAN. Are you, Midge?

MIDGE. Like everything.

MRS. HARTMAN. Then there's nothing more for me to say. *(Goes to dining room door)* —Except this, dear—we all love you very much and we'd do anything to make this—this coming-of-age easier. But you're on your own now. *(Exits.)*

(MIDGE, *alone, stays quietly tense for a moment, her head down. Then—very slowly—she raises her head and rises. There is a quick KNOCK at the Left 2 door.* MIDGE *hurriedly dabs her eyes, goes to door—opens it.* FREDDIE, *dressed for the dance, stands there, stiff and formal, and distant.)*

FREDDIE. I was summoned.

MIDGE. Oh, yes. Come in, Freddie. (FREDDIE *enters.)* Sit down, won't you?

FREDDIE. Make it snappy. *(Goes to sit in chair down Left.)* I'm going to the dance.

MIDGE. You're going to the dance without *Gabby?!*

FREDDIE. Stag. *(Bitterly)* Let her go with Tommy Litchfield.

MIDGE. *(Taking a deep breath)* Well—then why don't you go with Dodie Frazier?

FREDDIE. *(Starting)* Who?

MIDGE. Dodie Frazier—you used to take her everywhere.

FREDDIE. That is a gross exaggeration. I may have had a few dates—

MIDGE. *(Goes to table, Center, and picks up a photograph album; pages hastily)* I don't like to have to do this. *(Finds what she wants; rips it out of album.)* But feast your eyes on this. *(Extends picture.)* You and Dodie Frazier dancing cheek to cheek.

FREDDIE. That was years ago.

MIDGE. I know. At least six months. Freddie, Gabby has looked at Tommy Litchfield the way she looks at wallpaper for at least five months, maybe longer.

FREDDIE. She has? *(Rising)* —Say, do you think I've made a fool of myself?

MIDGE. I wouldn't be surprised. I know I have.

FREDDIE. You think Gabby'll—forgive and forget?

MIDGE. I've done my part. Give me the picture.

(KNOCK at door. MIDGE opens door. A MESSENGER BOY stands there holding box of flowers. MIDGE dashes back to FREDDIE.)

MIDGE. Give me a dime.

FREDDIE. *(Digging into pocket)* I guess our little conversation is worth it. *(Gives her coin. She dashes back to door; puts it in MESSENGER's hand.)*

MESSENGER. *(Off)* Thanks, Shorty.

(MIDGE *slams door violently. She comes down to Center table with flowers, searching for card.* FREDDIE *goes over to watch.* MIDGE *takes out card, and reads:*)

MIDGE. "For Carollyn, from—*Keith!*"
FREDDIE. Bet they're orchids.
MIDGE. But Freddie, don't you get it? Virginia thinks *she's* going with Keith!
FREDDIE. Oh-oh. Another wrench in the transmission!
MIDGE. *(With decision)* I've got to go see Buzz.
FREDDIE. Buzz? What's Buzz got to do with it?
MIDGE. This is vital. Don't you see?— Virginia won't have anyone to go with.
FREDDIE. *(Scratching his head)* Now you got *me* running the bases. I thought Buzz was on *your* wave length.
MIDGE. *(Sadly, tapping flower box)* He is. *(Pause)* I mean—well, he *was*.
FREDDIE. You change awfully fast, Midge.
MIDGE. No, I don't. *(Slowly)* I don't *think* I do. —Gosh, Freddie, I'm—I'm all crossroads and detours.—Look, do me a favor. Go find Buzz. Tell him —tell him he's needed and—well, tell him to hurry.
FREDDIE. *(Starts to go)* Okay!
MIDGE. And Freddie— (FREDDIE *pauses*) You better not tell him *I* sent for him. He m-might not come.
FREDDIE. Gee, Midge, I'm sorry.
MIDGE. *(Unhappy)* Get going.
FREDDIE. That's sort of—*noble*.

(FREDDIE *goes to Left 2 door and opens it just as* KEITH, *also dressed for the dance, is ready to knock.* KEITH *looks a little foolish for a minute, tapping on thin air. He has several dark bruises on his face.* FREDDIE *brushes by him.*)

MIDGE. Hello, Keith! *(Goes to stairs. Calling to* VIRGINIA*) Virginia!*
KEITH. *(Irascibly)* You got it wrong again.
MIDGE. Look at your face. Didn't you wash?
KEITH. You can't wash *that* off.
MRS. HARTMAN. *(Enters from dining room)* Edna's gone!
MIDGE. Good!
MRS. HARTMAN. *(With a look)* What!?
MIDGE. *(Going to Left 2 door)* Well, goodbye now. Gotta see a man about his wife. *(She is gone.)*
VIRGINIA. *(Comes down the stairs still wearing her everyday street clothes)* Oh, Keith, you're early.
MRS. HARTMAN. *(Going into sun parlor—still looking)* I can't understand where Edna would go.
KEITH. *(Answering* VIRGINIA*)* Just a trifle.—I—like to be on time.
VIRGINIA. I know. *(Sees flowers. Goes to them.)* And you've brought me flowers. Oh, Keith, you shouldn't have.
KEITH. *(Taking a step her way)* Well, you see those orchids—
VIRGINIA. Orchids! Oh, Keith, the *first* time!
KEITH. *(Embarrassed)* As a matter of fact, Virginia—
VIRGINIA. *(Has now taken card and the significance of it is written across her face)* Carollyn!
KEITH. Now you know I didn't exactly—I never have precisely—well, *asked* you.
VIRGINIA. *(Thunderstruck)* Keith Nolan! We talked about it *hundreds* of times. We've talked about it ever since Senior Play.
BUZZ. *(Left 2 door opens and* BUZZ, *also dressed for dance, bursts in)* What's the matter over here? *(He is breathless—he has been running.)*
KEITH. What are *you* doing here?
BUZZ. I came to go to the dance.
VIRGINIA *(Wailing)* With who—I mean, whom?

Buzz. *(Puzzled)* Why, Carollyn, I guess.
Virginia. Carollyn! You've *both* come to take *Carollyn!* I'm so wretched I could die! *(She throws herself on sofa, sobbing.)*

(Elliott *enters from dining room. Sees* Virginia. Buzz *and* Keith *are hovering over her, puzzled and gesturing helplessly.)*

Elliott. What did you do to her? *(Into* Keith's *face)* Listen, you, that's my sister.
Virginia. Go away.
Elliott. I will *not* go away. If either one of these two brutes have hit you—
Mr. Hartman. *(Off upstairs)* Please stop that wailing down there.
Virginia. What did he say?
Keith. He wants you to stop wailing like a banshee.
Virginia. *(Bursting into fresh and louder sobs)* You called me a *banshee!*
Keith. I did *not* call you a banshee.

(Carollyn *comes slowly down the stairs, not yet dressed for the dance.)*

Elliott. There you are.
Virginia. Who's that?
Buzz. It's Carollyn.
Virginia. *(Cries louder)* Ohhhhhh!

(Carollyn *remains on stairs and the three* Boys, *neglecting* Virginia, *go to* Carollyn, *facing her.)*

Keith. I think it's time we got this settled.
Buzz. Somebody's been sold short around here.
Elliott. Who *are* you going to the Prom with?

CAROLLYN. Now boys, you've got me all confused already.

VIRGINIA. *(Sitting up, realizing she's neglected)* You *ought* to be confused.

BUZZ. In about two minutes I'm gonna get out of this confounded house and stag it.

ELLIOTT. *(To* BUZZ*)* What's stagging it?

BUZZ. I mean I'm going by myself. I'm going to dance with every girl there.

VIRGINIA. Buzz Lindsay, that's a *fine* way to talk.

ELLIOTT. *(The dawn breaking)* You mean you can go to the Spring Prom with*out* a girl?!

BUZZ. And I don't think it's such a bad idea.

VIRGINIA. But a girl can't. The boys have all the privileges.

BUZZ. For Pete's sake, Virginia, stop that yapping and we'll get somewhere.

(VIRGINIA *cries.*)

ELLIOTT. Please desist. A logical, rational conclusion is never impossible.

KEITH. Please, Virginia—

CAROLLYN. *(Fiercely)* So you're all against her! *(The* BOYS *all turn, properly astonished)* You're behaving horribly, all of you. Virginia's my friend and I won't allow it.

KEITH. *Your* friend!—After the way you've treated her!

BUZZ. That's a nerve—you stepping up to bat!

ELLIOTT. I really must say, Carollyn, your defense is out of place at this point.

VIRGINIA. *(Rising)* Stop it! Stop it this instant, all of you! *(Directly to the three* BOYS*)* I won't have you talking to my guest this way.

BUZZ. Ohhh—
ELLIOTT. Well— } *(Together)*
KEITH. I say—

VIRGINIA. *(Crosses to stairs)* You're terrible. You're fiends. Casting aspersions on my house guest. *(Takes* CAROLLYN'S *hand)* Come, Carollyn. I'm sorry I couldn't introduce you to any *gentlemen* in this town.

(CAROLLYN *and* VIRGINIA, *heads high, go upstairs. The three Boys, left alone, look at each other, and then slowly take following seats:* ELLIOTT *down Left chair,* BUZZ *on sofa,* KEITH *in Center chair. They glance nervously at each other. Then three heads sinks onto three pairs of hands. They examine the floor for a moment. All three heads snap up at the same time.)*

BUZZ. This is—
KEITH. I never knew—   *(Together)*
ELLIOTT. Is that any way—

(Pause.)

ELLIOTT. *(Politely)* Go ahead.
KEITH. *(Equally polite)* I'm sorry.
BUZZ. *(Not to be outdone)* Beg pardon.

(Another pause.)

ELLIOTT. In books women always—
KEITH. I really don't have as much   *(Together)*
experience—

(They look at each other again. Pause.)

ELLIOTT. How do you feel, Keith?
KEITH. Like a wet sock. How's the eye?
ELLIOTT. Had beefsteak on it all afternoon.
KEITH. My ribs feel like red hot steel.
ELLIOTT. *(Proudly)* We lasted almost an hour.

Buzz. Aren't girls the darndest things?

Elliott. *(Acquiescing)* I have come to believe their psychology is based on their own reactions.

Keith. Their own reactions are twisted, don't you think?

Buzz. Sometimes I think it's nice—all those surprises they pull; but at other times it can be darned annoying.

Elliott. Tonight, for instance. For the weaker sex, they sure pack a wallop.

Keith. *(To* Elliott*)* Did you ask Carollyn to go with you?

Elliott. Yes. *(Belligerently)* What of it?

Keith. So did I.

(They Both *turn slowly to* Buzz.*)*

Buzz. I did too, but it wasn't my idea.

Elliott. *(Back on his old theme)* Women seem to think the shortest distance between two points is a circle.

Keith. *(To* Buzz*)* You didn't *want* to ask Carollyn?

Buzz. I think she's a drip.

Keith. *(To* Buzz*)* I always meant to tell you, Buzz. I didn't like the idea of taking Virginia away from you.

Buzz. That's all right; it was good for Virginia to play the field for a while.

Keith. She wasn't playing the field while she was with me!

Elliott. I thought we were talking about Carollyn.

Buzz. *(Picking up flowers)* I see you brought flowers.

Keith. Orchids. Went all over town to find them.

Buzz. I don't think if one girl just has gardenias, the other one ought to wear orchids, do you?

KEITH. Not if we all go together.
BUZZ. How much they worth?
KEITH. Two bucks apiece. There are two of them.
BUZZ. Four bucks. Can you take 'em back?
KEITH. I wouldn't do that.
BUZZ. Four bucks split three ways?—
ELLIOTT. One dollar thirty-three and one third cents.

(BUZZ *digs in pocket, places $1.50 on table, looks at* ELLIOTT. ELLIOTT *rises, digs in pocket, pulls out $1.00 and some change, crosses, lays the dollar and change on table. As he recrosses to chair:*)

ELLIOTT. Is this the way things are done? *(Sits)* This is all new to me.
KEITH. *(Scoops money into hand, jams it into pocket, picks up flowers)* What'll we do with them?
BUZZ. Give 'em here. I'll take care of them.
KEITH. But it's understood neither girl wears those flowers.
BUZZ. Check. *(Holds flowers in hand.)*
ELLIOTT. It's the democratic way, I guess.

(*The Left 2 door opens and* MIDGE, *escorting a confused* MR. FIELDS, *enters.* MIDGE *has been talking continuously.*)

MIDGE. —If a man doesn't stand on his *own* feet, he's lost. *You* should know that, Mr. Fields. Haven't you ever read James Thurber?
MR. FIELDS. But my dear child, I have been trying to explain for two blocks that you do *not* know my *wife*.
MIDGE. *(Seeing the* BOYS*)* Now these three young men will agree, won't you, boys?
KEITH. What?
ELLIOTT. What? } *(Together)*
BUZZ. What?

MIDGE. I've been trying to make clear to Mr. Fields that he'll never make the riffle if he lets any shemale lead him around with a ring in his nose.

MR. FIELDS. Young lady, I admire your realistic approach, but I don't like the way you describe things.

MIDGE. Ask the boys—they'll tell you a man can't be meek. He's got to stand up and fight for his rights. Isn't that right, fellows?

ELLIOTT. Don't ask us.

BUZZ. Outta my line.

KEITH. I'm a stranger here myself.

MR. FIELDS. At the office I'm perfectly all right,— but I've never been able to understand the members of the opposite sex.

BUZZ. *(Rising gallantly, gestures to* OTHERS *and to a place on the sofa)* Won't you join us, Mr. Fields?

MIDGE. *(Goes and leans against the desk)* I don't get this.

KEITH. We were discussing the same subject.

MIDGE. *(To* MR. FIELDS*)* Do bulls take orders from cows?

ELLIOTT. *(Sagely)* The Amazons were the only known women who could enforce their control— and look what happened to them when the Greeks came along!

MR. FIELDS. *(Softly)* What happened?

ELLIOTT. *(Rising)* The Greeks conquered them— *(Gestures)*—with love.

MR. FIELDS. I *tried* that.

MIDGE. I'll call my father. Now, Mr. Fields, remember what you said you'd *like* to be able to tell him. Well, just forget about your wife—and tell him you'll buy the trucks.

ELLIOTT. *(Going to stairs)* I'll send him down.

(BUZZ *and* KEITH, *rising together.)*

Buzz. Let's go take a walk.
Keith. I need some fresh air.
Midge. Oh, Buzz—
Buzz. Yes, Midge?
Midge. It's all right, Buzz—about the dance. I've arranged everything.
Buzz. *(Groaning)* Not again.
Midge. I'm not angry—or hurt—or anything.
Buzz. Good for you, kid. I'm not any of those things either. But I'm sure mixed up.
Midge. And please forget all those talks. I'm not ashamed of them—but—forget them, won't you?
Buzz. *(Going to her—comprehending)* If you say. *(He extends his hand.* Midge *takes it, vigorously.* Buzz *winces.)* Blisters still sore. *(Moves to Left 2 door)* You're all right, Midge.
Midge. Wish me luck, Buzz. Just for about ten minutes.
Buzz. I hope you don't get in deeper, that's all.
Midge. Where are you two going?

(Buzz *and* Keith *are at door.)*

Keith. To buy some gardenias.
Mr. Fields. *(To* Buzz*)* By the way, young man, I'm a terrible gardener myself.

(Buzz *and* Keith *go out Left 2.* Buzz *still carries orchid box.* Mr. Hartman *comes down the stairs.)*

Midge. Dad, look who came to see you.
Mr. Fields. *(Going to* Mr. Hartman*)* Mr. Hartman, this is a fruitless visit. My hands are tied.
Mr. Hartman. But I thought you *needed* those trucks?
Mr. Fields. I *do* need them. *(Gets a trifle angry)* I need them *immediately* and I need them *badly*. *(Gestures helplessly)* But Mrs. Fields—

Mr. Hartman. Oh, I see.

(The Left 2 door opens and Mrs. Fields, followed by Alan, who is dressed for dance, enters.)

Midge. If you give in now, Mr. Fields, you might as well cash in your chips.

(Alan crosses directly to Midge, who is now Right stage.)

Mrs. Field. *(Goes to her husband)* So you let that *child* talk you into coming here?
Alan. *(Reprimanding)* Mother!
Mrs. Fields. And you're apologizing for me. I know you are. And I won't have *that!*
Mr. Fields. Now Cecelia—
Midge. It's now or never, Mr. Fields. Do you want to act like Robert Benchley all your life?
Mrs. Fields. It seems to me you've caused quite enough disruptions, little girl—
Midge. *(To Mr. Fields—desperately)* I'll bet you've got indigestion. I'll bet you don't enjoy one meal in your own home—
Mr. Hartman. *(Remonstrating)* Midge!
Midge. *(Still to Mr. Fields—who listens)* All day long you work, you're important—then you come home and what do you find? *(Gestures)* Mrs. Fields.
Mrs. Fields. What's the matter with that?
Midge. It wouldn't *need* to be so dreadful. But look at your eyes—
Mrs. Fields. My *eyes?*

(Mr. Fields looks at Mrs. Fields' eyes, as though for the first time.)

Mr. Hartman. Midge, I forbid you to interfere—
Midge. Don't you see how important this is, Dad?

(To Mr. Fields) Take a good look, Mr. Fields. Those are the eyes that run your life.

MR. FIELDS. *(Turning to Midge)* You're badly mistaken, young lady—

ALAN. She's dead right, Pop—and you know it.

MRS. FIELDS. *(Scandalized)* Alan!

MR. FIELDS. *(Slumping,—to Alan)* So that's what *you* think?

ALAN. I'm sorry, Pop. I do. I agree with Midge.

MIDGE. Thanks, Alan. *(Then to Mrs. Fields)* —And now what does she want to do?—She's stepping into your office. (MR. HARTMAN *is silent now*) She's invading the—what you might say—last sanctuary of your—your— *(She can't think of a word.)*

ALAN. *(Helping out)* Your independence.

MRS. FIELDS. Come, Link. I have never heard so much adolescent babble in my life.

MR. FIELDS. *(Thinking)* My office? *(Fiercely, to Mrs. Fields)* What right have you in my office?

MRS. FIELDS. I'm not in your office. Let's get out of this house.

MIDGE. Spiritually she is.

MR. FIELDS. *(To Mrs. Fields)* Spiritually you've invaded my last sanctuary—

MRS. FIELDS. Link, control yourself. Remember what the doctor says.

MR. FIELDS. *(Even more fiercely)* That quack! I'm as healthy as I ever was. Just a little indigestion —because I don't enjoy my meals.—Well, from now on I'm going to enjoy every bite of food I eat. *(Into her face)* Hear that?—*Every* bite!

ALAN. Bravo, Pop!

MIDGE. *(Prompting)* This isn't the Dark Ages.

MR. FIELDS. No, it's not. *(Turns back to Mrs. Fields)* Do you hear that? This isn't the Dark Ages. This is the Twentieth Century. Men have been legally emancipated.

(Mrs. Hartman *enters from dining room—stops abruptly.*)

Mrs. Fields. *(Weakly)* Link, I've never seen you like *this* before.

Mr. Fields. I've never *been* like this before! *(Crosses to Mr. Hartman)* Mr. Hartman, I'll sign the contracts in the morning. *(Drunk with his independence)* I may even order a couple of extra trucks.

(Mrs. Hartman, *looking from one to the other, is trying to make out what is going on.*)

Mrs. Fields. *(Protesting weakly)* Link, I forbid—

Mr. Fields. *(To Mrs. Fields)* You *can't* forbid. I forbid you to ever forbid again.

Mrs. Hartman. Pardon me, but—

Mr. Fields. *(Seeing her for the first time, crosses. To Mrs. Hartman)* And Mrs. Hartman, if my wife ever makes one disparaging remark about your garden or your gardener, just let me know.

Mrs. Fields. *(One last burst)* What will you do?

Mr. Fields. *(Going back to her)* I'll make you resign from all the clubs in town.

Mrs. Fields. *(Subsiding)* Oh!

Mr. Fields. *(Not quite sure of his next move—clears throat)* Well,—

Midge. Mr. Fields, you're colossal!

Alan. Gosh, Dad, I can't believe it. Do you think we can go *fishing* on your vacation now?

Mrs. Fields. Link, that's just what I was going to suggest.

Mr. Fields. *Now* we're getting someplace. *(To* Midge*)* Thank you, young lady. I've had to go to the seashore every summer for fifteen years.

Midge. *(Happily)* I hope you catch all the bass in the world, Mr. Fields. *(Extends her hand.)*

MR. FIELDS. *(Taking her hand)* —And you send that Buzz—what's-his-name around to my office. I want to pay him his week's salary. I saw him *work*. *(Thinks)* No! *(Definitely)* Send him around to our house. *(To* MRS. FIELDS*)* Shall we go, Cecelia?

MRS. FIELDS. Yes. *(To* OTHERS*)* Well—all I can say is—I'm sorry. Perhaps it was all a mistake.

MRS. HARTMAN. I'm glad to hear you say it. You must come over to see my flowers sometime.

MRS. FIELDS. I shall, thank you. One learns from experience. *(Looks at* MR. FIELDS*)* —And I suppose mine is just beginning. *(Goes out Left 2.)*

MR. FIELDS. *(To* ALAN*)* You told me you wanted to ask that young lady *(Gestures to* MIDGE*)* to go to the dance with you. Well, ask her— *(Smiles to the assembled company)* You can't expect me to do *that* for you, can you? *(Goes.)*

(Pause. ALAN *goes to* MIDGE.*)*

ALAN. Well—uh—will you?

MIDGE. What?

ALAN. What he said—or you probably have a date already.

MIDGE. As a matter of fact, I do. *(Looks to her mother, who doesn't smile.* MIDGE *turns back to* ALAN *with determination)* No, I haven't. I'm not going to lie. I never *really* had a date for it and I've been forbidden to go to the dance.

(MR. *and* MRS. HARTMAN *exchange a glance.)*

ALAN. Oh! *(Looks to* MR. *and* MRS. HARTMAN*)* Well, I just thought I'd ask.

MIDGE. I'm sorry, Alan. I'd really like to go with you.

ALAN. You mean that?

MIDGE. Yes. Yes, I do. You've been so—swell. And we seem to agree on so many things.

ALAN. I've always thought that. May I—uh—could I come around tomorrow—just to see you?

MIDGE. Please do. But, Alan—I don't want you to think—well, it'll take some time for me to—recover, I'm afraid.

ALAN. Recover?

MIDGE. *(Brightly)* But maybe it won't after all—maybe it won't!

ALAN. Midge, I'm not going to the darn dance I'll stay here with you.

MIDGE. *(The beginning of something new)* Alan—!

(There is a general commotion at Left 2 door as GABBY, *now dressed brightly for dance, enters with* FREDDIE *holding her hand.* KEITH *and* BUZZ *follow.* BUZZ *now carries two flower boxes (the orchids in one hand and gardenias in the other) and* KEITH *carries one (gardenias.)*

GABBY. *(To* MIDGE*)* Got your boots laced, Jackson? The brawl is beginning.

MIDGE. *(Controlling her emotions)* I'm not going.

GABBY. You're not going?

MIDGE. *(Unsteadily)* I'm not going. But I'm glad to see you, Gabby.

MRS. HARTMAN. Is your dress pressed, Midge?

MIDGE. Mother!

MR. HARTMAN. Is it *pressed?*

MIDGE. Yes. *(Excitedly moving about, not knowing which way to turn)* I think so— Yes— Sure it is— Edna did— *(To* ALAN*)* —Gosh, Alan, I'll be happy to go with you. I don't know of anybody I'd rather— Wait for me! *(Dashes into dining room.)*

FREDDIE. Mrs. Hartman, you're a solid chick.

Mrs. Hartman. *(Uncertainly)* Thank you, Freddie.

Buzz. *(Going to* Mrs. Hartman*)* With our compliments. *(Extends orchid box.)*

Mrs. Hartman. *(Accepting)* For *me?*

Buzz. From three puzzled men.

Mrs. Hartman. *(Taking out orchids)* Orchids?!

Mr. Hartman. *(Smiling)* Look here. I don't know whether I should like this.

Keith. It's all right, Mr. Hartman. We admire your wife's stability.

Mrs. Hartman. Stability? I'm not sure *I* like that. *(Smiles.)*

(The dance MUSIC can be heard faintly in the distance; continues to end. Dining room door flies open and Midge *dashes pellmell across stage and upstairs, clutching dress to her. She now looks and acts about thirteen.)*

Mr. Hartman. *(To* Buzz*)* Three puzzled young men, you said. What are you puzzled about, Buzz?

Buzz. Virginia and Carollyn. They were practically crying like babies when they high-stepped out of here.

Mrs. Hartman. *(After pinning orchids on dress)* Crying? What's this? *(Starts for stairs.)*

Keith. Crying and gnashing their teeth and pulling their hair.

Buzz. Virginia's eyes won't look the same for days.

*(*Mrs. Hartman *is ascending stairs as* Virginia *and* Carollyn *appear on landing, arms linked.* Both *are beautifully gowned, smiling, gracious— young sophisticates ready for an evening at The Stork. Neither face shows any sign of worry or tears.)*

KEITH. Well—
BUZZ. Gosh— } *(Together)*
FREDDIE. Crying?—

CAROLLYN. *(Going to KEITH)* Ready, Curly?

VIRGINIA. *(Going to BUZZ, taking his arm)* All set, Buzz?

BUZZ. *(Exchanging a glance with KEITH)* What the—?

KEITH. *(Exchanging glances with BUZZ)* Guess—so—

GABBY. Let's light a firecracker. *(Sees ALAN for first time)* Oh, how ya, Alan?

ALAN. Hello!

FREDDIE. *(To ALAN)* Who you takin'?

(BUZZ *and* KEITH *are helping girls pin flowers to gowns.*)

ALAN. Midge.

FREDDIE. Midge?—But I thought—

GABBY. *(Interrupting with purpose)* That's choice!

FREDDIE. *(Blurting)* But he's a *senior!*

(At this point ELLIOTT, *not wearing glasses, dressed in new Tuxedo extremely well pressed, carrying a black felt hat, quite proper, enters on stairway.* MRS. HARTMAN, *now at foot of stairs, doesn't see him at first—neither do* OTHERS. GABBY *is first.)*

GABBY. Look at Aristotle!

(ALL *turn. General exclamations.* ELLIOTT, *not a bit embarrassed, looks them over a moment, blows on fingernails and rubs them on sleeve, lifts an eyebrow and starts down. At foot of stairs he meets his mother, who adjusts his tie. He draws away.)*

ELLIOTT. It's all right, Mother.

(MRS. HARTMAN *wisely withdraws her hand. He crosses in front of her and she makes a gesture toward him, catches herself. There are tears in her eyes.)*

FREDDIE. Who you takin', sharp lad?
ELLIOTT. I'm *stagging* it.
GABBY. Sure, give 'em all a break.
ELLIOTT. Precisely.
MR. HARTMAN. *(Smiling)* Where'd you get those duds, son?
ELLIOTT. If I need an encyclopedia, I can go to the library.

(MR. HARTMAN'S *mouth drops open.)*

VIRGINIA. Your encyclopedia money!?
ELLIOTT. *(Going to Left 2 door)* I don't think I'll need it now. *(Dons hat)* I intend to write about *young* people. I'll gather my material first hand— *(Gives the hat a smart little tap)* —starting *tonight*.
CAROLLYN. And I'm forgiven?
ELLIOTT. For what? *(He is the man of the world.)* For making me see what a fool I've been? Well, I couldn't write unless I knew heartbreak—and you know what the poet said:—

"Nay, let us walk from fire unto fire
From passionate pain to deadlier delight—
I am too young to live without desire,
Too young art thou to *waste* this summer's night!"

(He goes out.)
MRS. HARTMAN. *(Weakly)* Jeff—

Mr. Hartman. I'll be double darned!

(Mrs. Hartman *crosses to* Mr. Hartman, *down Right near desk.*)

Gabby. Listen to that music!

(*A KNOCK at Left 2 door.* Virginia *opens it.* Messenger Boy *stands there.*)

Messenger Boy. Telegram for Mrs. Hartman. (*Sees them all dressed up.* Virginia *takes telegram; crosses to* Mrs. Hartman. Messenger Boy *looks the* Boys *and* Girls *over.*) Orchids and telegrams and everything—swank shindig, huh? (*He goes.*)
Mrs. Hartman. (*Reading*) Oh!
Mr. Hartman. What, dear?
Mrs. Hartman. It's from Edna!
Carollyn. The maid?
Mrs. Hartman. Listen: (*Reads*) "Clancy and I hitched. Stop. If you want me back you must take Clancy too. Stop. Back from honeymoon in two weeks. Stop. Tell Midge it was a perfect idea. Signed—Edna and Clarence"!
Mr. Hartman. (*A trifle grimly*) Midge again
Virginia. Here she comes now.

(All *turn.* Midge *appears on landing. She is now quite the young lady. Her scrubbed shiny look is gone. Her hair is caught behind her ears becomingly. She wears a radiant expression. The transformation leaves the room breathless.* Midge *has a white envelope in her hand.*)

Mrs. Hartman. (*Starting toward stairs*) Child—

(Mr. Hartman *restrains her. He too is openmouthed.*)

ALAN. Midge, you look—like—a—swell!
MIDGE. Thank you, Alan. Is everyone ready?
FREDDIE. Ready, willing, and *(Does a dance step)* let the dance floor feel your leather! *(Takes GABBY's arm.)*
MIDGE. Oh, Carollyn! *(Gives her envelope)* These are yours. I had them developed for you.
CAROLLYN. *(Goes to take envelope)* Thank you, Midge. You're a dear. *(Goes to Center table, picks up the candid camera, hangs it around MIDGE's neck as she speaks)* Gratefully yours, Midge.
MIDGE. Do you mean it?
KEITH. Ready, Carollyn?

(CAROLLYN joins him and they go out Left 2.)

VIRGINIA. Have a good time, sis.
BUZZ. Save me a dance, kid. *(WARN Curtain.)*
MIDGE. Perhaps one. *(Takes ALAN's hand)* The others are all taken.

(VIRGINIA and BUZZ go out.)

FREDDIE. We're off to see the Wizard.

(GABBY and FREDDIE go out. MIDGE goes to her mother, gives her a light kiss and a quick hug.)

MIDGE. 'Night, Mother. *(Same business with her father.)* 'Night, Dad. And thanks—both of you—thanks so much! *(Rejoins ALAN and they go to Left 2 door. At door, she stops abruptly, turns to her parents—a surprised expression on face)* It's over! Vacation's all over—and I haven't done a thing!

(She and ALAN go out, closing the door. Pause.)

MR. HARTMAN. She hasn't done a thing.

Mrs. Hartman. —Just grown right up and away from us, that's all.

Mr. Hartman. What's that?

Mrs. Hartman. Nothing. Just thinking. Well, let's sit down and enjoy our "stability," Jeff.

Mr. Hartman. *(Bending over to smell the orchid)* Well, that's the end of spring vacation—for another year. You know, they're darned attractive kids—even if it did take storms and hurricanes to bring them up.

Mrs. Hartman. Orchids don't smell, Jeff.

Mr. Hartman. Oh— But thank the Lord it's over.

Mrs. Hartman. Over? What do you mean? It's just begun.

Mr. Hartman. Just begun?

Mrs. Hartman. Spring, you oaf. *(Unconsciously she bends over to smell the orchid which doesn't smell.)*

Mr. Hartman. But listen to me, Louise— *(Curtain is descending)* Next year, come spring vacation, by all the unlucky parents of the next generation, I'm going to go fishing—

BUT THE CURTAIN HAS FALLEN

AND CAME THE SPRING

PROPERTY PLOT

Decorative Properties:
    Two mirrors.
    Two colorful prints, framed.
    Ash trays, pipe rack.
    Drapes on all windows, also glass curtains.
    Several vases of flowers, one on radio.
    Books and book ends.
    Bric-a-brac on desk.
    Hanging bookcase.

Set Properties:
    Desk, down R.
    Straight chair behind desk.
    Telephone on desk.
    Occasional table below the landing.
    Lamp on table.
    Sofa at Left Center.
    Drum table to the Right of sofa.
    Lamp on table.
    Lounge chair next to table.
    Waste basket next to desk.
    Lounge chair down L. in the corner.
    Radio between the outside and dining room doors L.

Also Odd for Act One:
  Card table.
  A straight chair.

HAND PROPERTIES

ACT ONE

Tray with silver for two, dishes, linens, cream and sugar, 2 glasses of orange juice, marmalade, muffins in covered container, toast, butter and cereal on card table, EDNA.
Newspaper, L., CLANCY.
Box camera, R., MIDGE.
Paper and pencil on desk, MIDGE.
Hat and coat, R., MR. HARTMAN.
Coffee percolator and coffee, L., EDNA.
Handbag, hat, gloves, R., VIRGINIA.
Books, papers, notebooks, L., ELLIOTT.
Tray with cup of tea, a slice of toast, silver, and napkin, L., EDNA.
Tray with two cups and saucers, silver for two, napkins, two bowls of cereal, two glasses of orange juice, a plate on which are two eggs and bacon, and an empty plate for muffins, etc., for ELLIOTT, L., EDNA.
Typewriter, L., ELLIOTT.
Wide-brimmed hat, smock, gloves, R., MRS. HARTMAN.
Keys in purse, VIRGINIA.
Book, R., ELLIOTT.
Two small and two large pieces of airplane luggage, L., KEITH.
Candid camera, L., CAROLLYN.
Cover-alls, R., ELLIOTT.

ACT TWO—SCENE I

Newspaper on desk, MIDGE.

PROPERTY PLOT

Pipe and tobacco in jacket pocket, Mr. Hartman.
Hat on chair, l., Mr. Hartman.
Hat, purse and gloves on table to the r., Mrs. Hartman.
Typewriter, r., Elliott.
Envelope in pocket, Christine.
Newspaper, l., Mr. Hartman.

SCENE II

Fourteen or fifteen snapshots in pocket, Midge.
Candid camera on Center table, Midge.
Pipe, l., Elliott.
Hats and coats, l., Mr. and Mrs. Hartman.
Newspapers and magazines laying around room, Mrs. Hartman.
Handkerchief, r., Virginia.
Lounging robe, r., Mr. Hartman.
Lounging robe, r., Carollyn.
Flash bulb and camera, r., Midge.

SCENE III

Water glasses on floor, Elliott.
Two golf balls in golf trousers, Elliott.
Golf club, Elliott.
Pipe, Elliott.
Towel on head, eyelash curler, r., Virginia.
Fourteen or fifteen snapshots, l., Midge.
Apple, l., Midge.
Hat, purse, gloves, l., Mrs. Hartman.
Clarinet, l., Buzz.
Ice cubes in a towel, r., Virginia.
Newspaper, l., Mr. Hartman.

ACT THREE

Newspaper, l., Mr. Hartman.

Ice bag, R., ELLIOTT.
Handkerchief in pocket, MIDGE.
Photograph album on Center table, MIDGE.
Box of orchids with card and pin in box, L., MESSENGER BOY.
Dime in pocket, FREDDIE.
Loose change and bills in pockets, ELLIOTT and BUZZ.
Two extra flower boxes with gardenias and pins in each, L., BUZZ and KEITH.
Formal gown, L., MIDGE.
Telegram, L., MESSENGER BOY.
White envelope, R., MIDGE.
Candid camera on Center table, CAROLLYN.

SOUND EQUIPMENT

Telephone bell.
Typewriter.
Auto horn.
Swing music records heard on radio.
Dance music to be heard in distance.

AND CAME THE SPRING

LIGHT PLOT

General lighting cheerful and bright. For the daylight scenes (Act One and Act Two, Scene III) it is suggested that a sunlight stream in at window and outside door. This can be accomplished by using the proper media in two spots or floods placed to throw light *through* window and *across* door up L. For the night scenes (Act Two, Scenes I and II, and Act Three) these media should be replaced by steel blue colors for moonlight effect.

Moonlight floods or spots remain on throughout all night scenes. Actual *dimming* is not necessary. When a lamp is switched off, the general intensity can be cut down to show that light has been turned off in room. One simple way to avoid any difficulty is to attempt no lessening of light until last light is turned off in each scene—then *Black Out* all except moonlight.

LIGHT CUES

Act One, Scene I—
  Cue: MRS. HARTMAN—"I imagine so."
  General lights *dim* when she turns off lamp up R.
  Cue: MIDGE—"Goodnight, Mother."
  General lights *dim* when MRS. HARTMAN turns off lamp C.

Cue: MIDGE—"But maybe young people are older younger nowadays."

MIDGE turns out all *Lights* at switch on wall near door, up L. Black out everything except *Moonlight* floods or spots through window and open door. This stands until *Curtain.*

Act Two, Scene III—

Cue: ELLIOTT—"I didn't want to come out before."

General lights *dim* when MIDGE turns out lamp, C.

Cue: MIDGE—"In her room—polishing her technique."

General lights *dim* when MIDGE turns out lights, at wall switch, up L.

Cue: CAROLLYN—"You don't know how everyone's been treating me."

Black out everything except *Moonlight* floods or spots through window. This stands until Curtain.

THE AUTHORS

Marrijane and Joseph Hayes, the authors of *And Came The Spring,* are a young married couple living in New York City, where they have become ardent and critical theatregoers. Both have written other plays and short pieces, about which they will reveal little, but *And Came The Spring* is the first comedy for amateurs which they have submitted to any publisher.

Mrs. Marrijane Hayes first took an active interest in the theatre while attending Butler University, Indianapolis. She has subsequently acted, designed sets and costumes, and performed all of the other jobs incident to theatre production in community, educational, and summer theatres in the Midwest. She steadfastly contends that none of the characters in the play resembles her in the least; she admits she might have known a Mrs. Hartman at some time, but declines to say when or where. She also willingly admits that several other characters in the play were inspired by the comic ideas behind many of James Thurber's cartoons.

As director of the Drama Loan Service of Indiana University and member of the staff for several years, Joseph Hayes has had more than ample opportunity to study the amateur theatre in all of its aspects. His directorial and acting work in various theatres in the Midwest has provided a practical background. With this knowledge of needs and requirements, he has approached the job of playwriting for the amateur field in a positive and practical manner. He likes plays of all types in all forms and will admit no preferences, "as long as it's a good play and honest to the author's intent, whether that is commercial or aesthetic—authors shouldn't kid themselves."

AND CAME THE SPRING

PUBLICITY THROUGH YOUR LOCAL PAPERS

The press can be an immense help in giving publicity to your productions. In this belief we submit a number of suggested press notes which may be used either as they stand or changed to suit your own ideas and submitted to the local press.

If you are a harassed father, an amused mother, if you are a son or a daughter or a brother or a sister—in short, if you belong to a typical American family, you may find yourself being humorously portrayed on the stage of the ———— Theatre next week. The ———— Players (School) have chosen the new American comedy, *And Came The Spring*, for their next production.

The play tells the ingenious and gay story of the Hartmans and their comic and sometimes poignant experiences during the first hectic week of Spring. There is a possibility that you may have in your family as charming and exuberant a hovden as Midge, just sixteen, who causes all the comic trouble. While Midge has characteristics of every girl her age all over the world, she is still unique. She starts tornadoes, she disrupts romances, she falls in love with the wrong boy, she drops a bombshell into her father's business—Midge is a whirlwind. But the Hartmans love her and so will the audiences at the ———— Theatre next week.

The box-office has announced that tickets are now on sale, and large audiences are planning to rock with laughter at *And Came the Spring*. Be sure to make your reservations early.

****

There are plays and plays about modern American families. Each is a little different. Each serves its own purpose. In the past some of the most popular and most frequently produced plays have fallen into this category. But only occasionally do two authors approach the subject with the freshness, insight, and humor which characterizes *And Came The Spring*, the new comedy by Marrijane and Joseph Hayes.

Today, when comedy is especially needed in the world, these two authors have supplied it lavishly, all the while preserving the naturalness and heightening the color of their interesting characters. It has often been said that all good comedy springs from character; although *And Came The Spring* is full of unexpected and highly diverting situations, the emphasis on truth and character is foremost.

Life is made up of poignancy as well as laughter—and what is more filled with both of these qualities than first love? What has more universal appeal? Here is a moving as well as amusing picture of a first love which begins an avalanche of complications calculated to win the approval of even the saddest member of any audience.

Written with sensitivity, *And Came The Spring* skims along blithely as it relates the amusing story of the Hartmans when the youngest girl in the family finds herself enormously successful (for a while) in her manipulations of other lives for her own ends. The story builds to deft and hilarious climaxes, all the while it keeps its eye on the human traits and emotions motivating the characters.

Are young people actually more irresponsible today, because of their seemingly flippant and easy-going manner, than was the youth in other times? That is the theme of *And Came The Spring*. The ———— Players of ———— will present this new comedy at ———— on ————. The play will throw new light on the question in a manner which is designed to entertain.

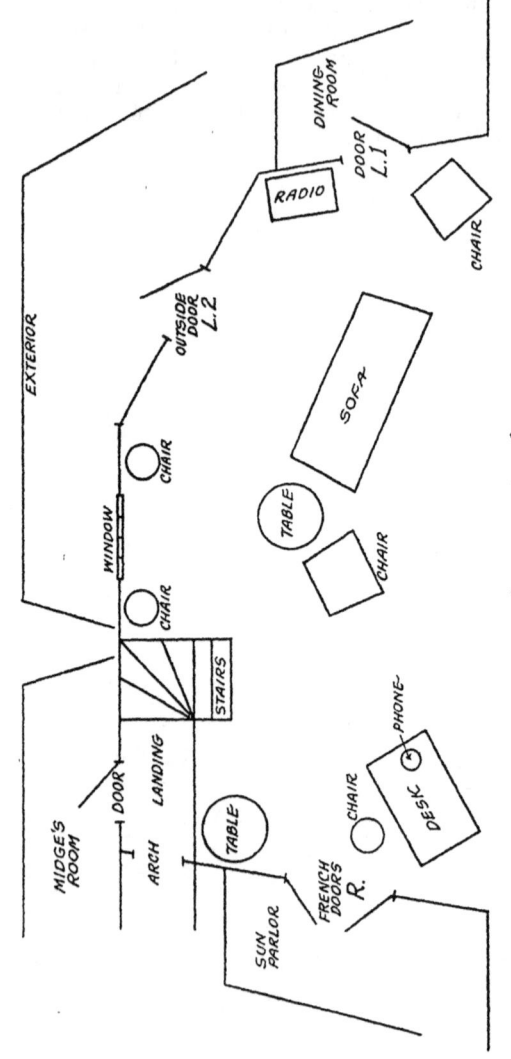

OTHER TITLES AVAILABLE FROM SAMUEL FRENCH

QUIET SUMMER
Marrijane Hayes and Joseph Hayes

Farce / 8m, 10 f / Interiors

James Clark plans to spend a peaceful summer concentrating on getting elected president of his country club, a first step toward becoming District Attorney in the fall. Uncle Jimmie's plans go astray when Pamela, 17, and Sonny, 15, arrive. He wins his election with inventive help from the kids, but they also all but wreck James' romance and turn the house upside down.

www.ingramcontent.com/pod-product-compliance
Lightning Source LLC
Chambersburg PA
CBHW070643300426
44111CB00013B/2237